Working Effectively With Your Teaching Assistant

Other titles from Bloomsbury Education

Feel Free to Smile: The behaviour management survival guide for new teachers by Nikki Cunningham-Smith

How to be an Outstanding Primary Teaching Assistant by Emma Davie

The Emotionally Intelligent Teacher: Enhance teaching, improve wellbeing and build positive relationships by Niomi Clyde Roberts

The Teacher Journal: Bitesize CPD and reflective activities for a successful school year by Naomi Barker

What Every Teacher Needs to Know: How to embed evidence-informed teaching and learning in your school by Jade Pearce

You Got This!: Thriving as an early career teacher with Mr T by Andrew Taylor

Working Effectively With Your Teaching Assistant

A handbook for primary teachers

Sara Alston

BLOOMSBURY EDUCATION
LONDON OXFORD NEW YORK NEW DELHI SYDNEY

BLOOMSBURY EDUCATION
Bloomsbury Publishing Plc
50 Bedford Square, London, WC1B 3DP, UK
29 Earlsfort Terrace, Dublin 2, Ireland

BLOOMSBURY, BLOOMSBURY EDUCATION and the Diana logo are trademarks of Bloomsbury Publishing Plc

First published in Great Britain, 2023 by Bloomsbury Publishing Plc

Text copyright © Sara Alston, 2023
Illustrations (ant, mouse, cat, lion, elephant, p.183) copyright © Shutterstock, 2023
Illustrations (hand, p. 114) copyright © Rachael Reeves, 2023

Sara Alston has asserted her right under the Copyright, Designs and Patents Act, 1988, to be identified as Author of this work

Bloomsbury Publishing Plc does not have any control over, or responsibility for, any third-party websites referred to or in this book. All internet addresses given in this book were correct at the time of going to press. The author and publisher regret any inconvenience caused if addresses have changed or sites have ceased to exist, but can accept no responsibility for any such changes

All rights reserved. No part of this publication may be reproduced or transmitted in any form or by any means, electronic or mechanical, including photocopying, recording, or any information storage or retrieval system, without prior permission in writing from the publishers

A catalogue record for this book is available from the British Library

ISBN: PB: 978-1-4729-9256-7; ePDF: 978-1-4729-9254-3; ePub: 978-1-4729-9255-0

2 4 6 8 10 9 7 5 3 1 (paperback)

Typeset by Newgen KnowledgeWorks Pvt. Ltd., Chennai, India
Printed in Great Britain by CPI Group (UK) Ltd, Croydon, CR0 4YY

MIX
Paper | Supporting responsible forestry
FSC
www.fsc.org FSC® C013604

To find out more about our authors and books visit www.bloomsbury.com and sign up for our newsletters

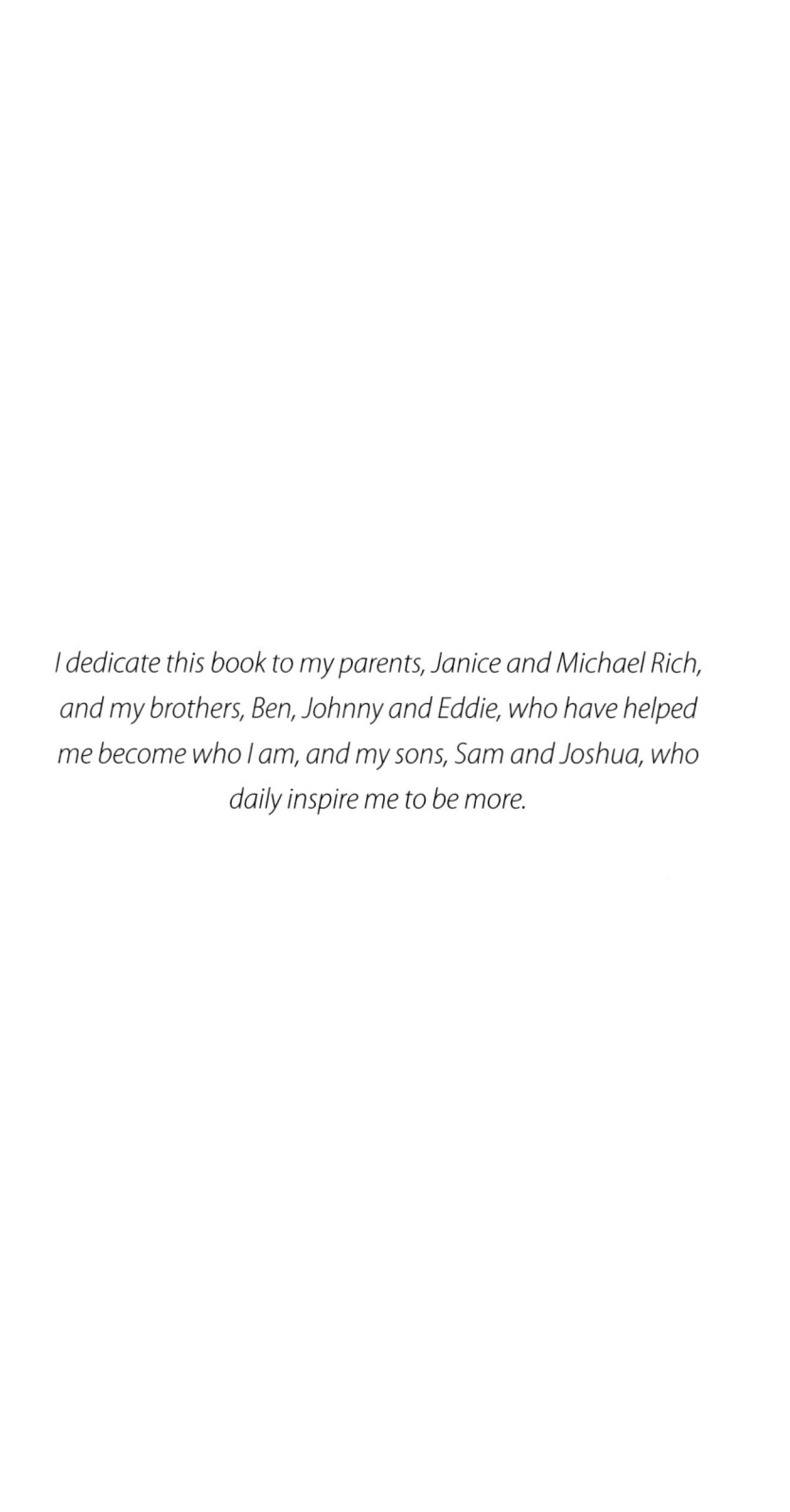

I dedicate this book to my parents, Janice and Michael Rich, and my brothers, Ben, Johnny and Eddie, who have helped me become who I am, and my sons, Sam and Joshua, who daily inspire me to be more.

Contents

Preface ix

  Introduction: The ten challenges of working with TAs and why they are no one's fault 1

1 Understanding what you want your TA to do in the classroom 21

2 Focus on support for children with SEND 45

3 Supporting home–school communication 69

4 Supporting learning in the classroom 91

5 Support throughout the lesson 109

6 Interventions 133

7 Sharing planning and feedback 153

8 Supporting with behaviour: consistency imbued with flexibility 171

9 Pulling it all together by placing communication at the heart of all we do 197

Glossary 211
References 213
Index 217

Preface

I am in the odd position of writing a book using a job title – teaching assistant or TA – that it would not be my choice to use. I use it for clarity as it is the job title in most common usage for support staff working within the classroom in England. It is used in government guidance and most of the research in this area. However, when I refer to a TA, I do not mean a 'teacher's assistant' whose role is purely to support the teacher as a kind of personal assistant by providing admin support and so on, but an LSA, a learning support assistant – the job title I prefer! This is the role that the majority of classroom support assistants carry out. Their primary role is to support children and their learning, though they may do this in different ways and under different guises. Their role may include assisting the teacher but their focus is and should be on the children and their needs and learning, not those of the teacher.

I am aware that there is a huge array of job titles in use in British schools to describe the amazing people who are not teachers working to support children in our classrooms. Some reflect specific qualifications or areas of practice; others the ways staff are used in a particular school. They may also reflect variations in the expectations placed on staff or the roles they carry out, but not always. The job titles I have found include:

- CA – classroom assistant
- BSA – behaviour support assistant
- ETA – education teaching assistant
- SNA – special needs assistant
- INA – individual needs assistant
- ANA – additional needs assistant
- Cover supervisor

- HLTA – high level teaching assistant
- ELSA – emotional literacy support assistant
- LM – learning mentor
- AT – associate teacher
- PA – pastoral assistant
- Consequences gatekeeper
- Associate tutor
- Bilingual support assistant
- NNEB – National Nursery Examination Board (qualified)
- UT – unqualified teacher
- NA – nurture assistant

In addition to any questions over the job title 'TA', I ask for forgiveness for using the term 'your TA'. This is not to imply either a hierarchy where teachers are superior to TAs or that TAs are owned by teachers. If writing from a TA's perspective, I would equally write 'your teacher'. I merely mean the TA or teacher that you work with and with whom you share your room and class.

Throughout this book, when I refer to 'parents', I mean parents, carers and guardians – anyone with caring responsibilities for children.

Throughout the text, I have included the stories of teachers, TAs and children. All of these are fictional, though the inspiration comes from those I have had the privilege to work with and who have taught me so much.

Though I am the author of this book and accept responsibility for any errors in it, I was supported by many other people. Particular thanks should go to my publishers Hannah Marston (now at BERA), Emily Badger and Cathy Lear at Bloomsbury and to those who read the book at various stages, including Michael Purches, Ben Slater, Sue Allingham and Howard Webber.

I need to also thank the staff, especially the TAs and LSAs with whom I have worked in a range of schools over the last 35+ years, particularly at Pyrcroft, Leatherhead Trinity and Pirbright Village Primary Schools.

Specific thanks go to Sue Allingham and Grace Durdle for being amazing resources of all things Early Years, Ruth Swailes for the word 'outvention', Chiara Dow for her ideas about the intervention monitoring form, Rachael Reeves for work on some of the images in the text, the Surrey Behaviour Support specialist teachers for shaping and supporting my thoughts about behaviour management, and those I worked with in nurture groups, particularly Melissa Heard and Carolanne Gale. Last, but not least, Wendy Howells, because friendships made in the classroom can last a lifetime.

How to use this book

While this book will include some theory and background information, its focus is on practical advice and strategies based on real classroom practice. To support this, I have included:

- lots of case studies and 'If this isn't working ... try this' examples to provide links to practice in real classrooms
- personal stories from my time as a teacher, school leader and education consultant
- quotes from teachers and TAs
- an occasional 'Extra useful information' box.

Each chapter ends with a summary, including:

- key points to remember
- things to discuss with senior leaders – because we don't work on our own in schools and there are things we need to share and be supported with by others
- things to think about – ideas to reflect on and discuss with colleagues

- things that work really well – simple things that others have tried and that work.

At the end of the book is a glossary of some of the key terms and abbreviations used throughout the book.

Introduction: The ten challenges of working with TAs and why they are no one's fault

'Sometimes, we end up blaming ourselves and our TAs for things that we can't control, rather than working to improve what we can.'

Teacher

Sharing the cape

In recent years, we have been reminded that 'not all heroes wear capes'. This was a key message of the 'Clap for Carers' during the UK's first Covid lockdown in the spring of 2020. Teachers were named as key workers. However, using 'teachers' as a shorthand for all school staff disregards the more than a third of school staff who are not teachers. While some are administrative, site and catering staff, the majority are teaching assistants. It was often they who kept schools running during the Covid pandemic – providing the on-site teaching for vulnerable pupils and the children of key workers while the teachers developed and taught an online curriculum. It was an example of the teamwork that underlies the good practice in so many classrooms. If teachers are heroes, so are their TAs. The 'cape' needs to be shared.

Yet TAs and their role and impact are largely ignored by many thinking about schools. The Ofsted inspection handbook in 2021 (since updated) included just *one* reference to teaching assistants in 49 pages: that observations of pupils' behaviour and attitudes to learning in lessons should include 'how well pupils respond to teaching assistants and other support staff'. The 2022 SEND Review (DfE, 2022b, p. 43) recognised that 'Teaching assistants play a key role in supporting children and young people with SEND to access learning in the classroom' and promised more on their effective use and deployment as part of the proposed national standards for SEND. But it gave no further details.

When TAs are considered, the focus is on school leaders and how to deploy TAs or in the hundreds of books on how to be a good TA. There is very little for class teachers on how to work with TAs and manage these vital classroom relationships. It is assumed that this will happen by magic. Such guidance as exists tends to focus on remediation, problem-solving and intervention when relationships go wrong, rather than on a proactive approach to equip teachers with the skills and understanding they need to work effectively with their TAs to promote learning.

In this book I am going to take the teacher's point of view, focusing on how you as a teacher can work effectively with your TAs, so that you can become the leader of a team in your classroom, 'sharing the cape' and supporting children's learning. We are going to start by considering some of the challenges to effective teacher/TA working relations, which, to be clear, are the fault of neither.

Challenge 1: The assumption that if you can manage children, you can manage adults

There is an implicit belief within teacher training and within schools that those who can manage a class of children can also manage an adult or adults, implying that managing children and deploying staff effectively are the same thing. They are not. Taking the same approach to working with adult colleagues as you do to organising a class of children is a quick route to disaster.

The Department for Education (DfE) guidance for teachers and teacher training provides little information for teachers on how to manage their TAs.

- The Teachers' Standards (2011) gives a single bullet point under 'Standard 8: Fulfil wider professional responsibilities' (p. 13), which includes 'deploy support staff effectively', without any explanation or further detail.
- The ITT Core Content Framework (DfE, 2019b), which reflects the Teachers' Standards, includes a little more guidance. It has six mentions of teaching assistants in 49 pages. These focus on trainees making 'effective use of teaching assistants and other adults in the classroom under the supervision of expert colleagues' (p. 20).

  Further, under Standard 8, it notes 'Teaching assistants (TAs) can support pupils more effectively when they are prepared for lessons by teachers, and when TAs supplement rather than replace support from teachers.' (p. 29) It goes on to suggest that trainees should discuss with their mentor and expert colleagues how to share the intended lesson outcomes with TAs ahead of lessons. Furthermore, it covers how to ensure that support provided by TAs is additional to, rather than a replacement for, support from the teacher. This should include preparing TAs for lessons.
- The Early Career Framework (DfE, 2019a) merely repeats the information from the Teachers' Standards and ITT Core Content Framework. It notes that teachers should 'Build effective working relationships by seeking ways to support individual colleagues and working as part of a team' (p. 24).

This feels like quite a lot of stating the obvious 'what', but little of the 'how'. The result is that many newly qualified teachers don't feel confident about the effective deployment of support staff (Ginni et al., 2018).

> **Case study**
>
> Samira was excited to be finally appointed to her first teaching role, though she was nervous as it was away from her home town, where she had done her teacher training and been to uni. On her visit to her new school, Samira was delighted to meet her new TA, who reminded her of her mother and promised to show her the ropes. It was only a brief meeting. As the summer went on and the start of term approached, Samira became increasingly anxious about how she was to get her TA to do what she wanted. She could not imagine telling this woman what to do any more than she could imagine directing her mother around her own house. She realised that she lacked even the vocabulary to begin to do this or to form a relationship where she and the TA could work as a team under her direction rather than under the TA's.

Like Samira, many newly qualified teachers are asked to work with TAs who have far more classroom experience than them and may be many years their senior. When the relationship works, teachers can find having a TA from a different generation useful, as they can share their experiences and offer different perspectives and approaches. Though it can be difficult, both TAs and teachers can and do learn from each other.

Challenge 2: The role of the TA has developed by stealth

Although there have always been support staff in classrooms, no one planned for the role that TAs currently take in the mainstream classroom. In Victorian schools, there were senior pupils and random others who conducted much of the teaching, under the supervision of a teacher, who often sat at the front with little interaction with up to a hundred children. More recently, there were parent helpers, who mainly helped with art and heard children read. In paid roles, there were a small number of ancillary staff who undertook general roles related to the smooth running of the school – filing, medical care, general tidying, maintaining the library and making the head's coffee. These people were not trained to or expected to carry out any kind of teaching role. Their role was to assist teachers, not promote or support learning in more than a minimal way.

Two major changes over the last half century have led to TAs' current role in mainstream classrooms, even though neither change was directly related to the role of the TA.

1. Changes in SEND

Until the Warnock Report in 1978, children with special needs were regarded as handicapped.[1] They were largely excluded from mainstream schools and placed in special schools and institutions. The Warnock Report changed the educational landscape and started the move to increased inclusion in mainstream schools. These changes were enshrined in the 1981 Education Act, which made it clear that all children should be educated in mainstream classes where possible. It replaced the term 'handicapped' with 'special educational needs' to describe those with:

a) significantly greater difficulty in learning than the majority of others of the same age

b) a disability that prevents or hinders them from making use of facilities of a kind generally provided for others of the same age in mainstream schools.

This promoted inclusion and led to a rapid increase in the number of children with special needs being taught in mainstream schools.

---

[1] The ten categories of 'handicap' defined by the 1944 Education Act were: 'blind, partially sighted, deaf, delicate, diabetic, educationally subnormal, epileptic, maladjusted, physically handicapped and speech defect'.

By the time of the SEND Code of Practice (DfE, 2015), this had developed into the current four areas of special needs and the two-level graduated response – SEN Support and EHCP (education, health and care plan) – supported by a SENCo.

> ### Personal story
>
> *When I started teaching in 1987 in an Inner London junior school, I had no children identified with special needs in my class. Looking back, however, I can identify several who would now meet the criteria, as they needed support 'different and additional to' that of their classmates, and there were two who needed to follow a completely differentiated curriculum. I did not have any TA support, though over the years I did manage to recruit a few parent helpers who heard readers and supervised the use of the computer.*
>
> *During my time at the school, there was only one child in the school who was identified as having special needs. She spent little time in lessons and went on to a special school.*
>
> *It was not until the mid-1990s, when I was working in a school with an attached special needs unit and a large number of children with significant special needs, that I had a TA in my classroom on a regular basis.*
>
> *Fast forward to 2006, I had eight children with statements (the precursor of EHCPs) for autism and a wheelchair user in my class of 24 children, and a staff team of seven TAs across the week (not all full-time).*

Over time, the employment and support of a TA has become, in many classrooms, the default form of support for children with a high level of SEND, particularly an EHCP.

2. The raising standards and workload agendas

From the 1980s onwards, alongside the reframing of the approach to SEND, there has been an increased emphasis on raising educational attainment, leading to the implementation of the National Curriculum from 1989 and the birth of Ofsted in 1992. These increased the pressures on school staff, and fed into a growing concern about teachers' recruitment, retention and workload.

These concerns led to 'The National Agreement' (ATL et al., 2003) between the government, employers and school workforce unions, aimed at tackling concerns about teachers' workload and stress. It established expectations for 'the increased use of staff who are not qualified teachers to work in a range of teaching and teaching support roles' (Nash, 2014, p. 15). It even included a list of 25 administrative and clerical tasks to be passed from teachers to support staff. This led to an increase in support staff in schools – not just TAs, but also administration, site and finance staff – and the introduction of PPA (preparation, planning and assessment) time.

Challenge 3: The role of a TA is not clear

In response to the concerns about inclusion, standards and teacher workload, TAs have moved from being a 'mums' army' who helped in classrooms to paid staff. The number of TAs increased from 79,000 in 2000, (DfE, 2015) to 265,167 in 2019/2020 – a 336 per cent increase in 20 years (Gov.uk, 2021). TAs are now regarded as an integral and important part of the school staff. A quick survey on Twitter found TAs described as:

- 'Worth their weight in gold'
- 'Beyond amazing'
- 'Pretty awesome'.

TAs have many different roles, both those directly involved in learning (such as supporting children with SEND, running interventions, giving additional input to small groups or helping with reading and phonics) and non-pedagogical roles (e.g. delivering speech therapy, supporting children with SEMH (social, emotional and mental health) needs, phoning parents, marking times tables tests, gathering resources, doing playground duties, dealing with first aid, managing lost property and much more).

> ### Personal story
>
> *I was recently visiting a large primary school to conduct a review of TA deployment. The head took me on a tour of the school. As we walked, I asked how they saw the role of TAs in the school. He replied, 'They support learning.' I inquired how they did that. He replied, 'Well, you know, they kind of support and do things.'*
>
> *The head had no clear idea what 23 – roughly half – of his staff did.*

The ambiguity about the role of TAs is reflected in the range and variety of job titles held by members of this staff group (see the preface for a list of some of these). Also, there are many staff who hold multiple roles within a school or move frequently between roles.

Case study

Laura first started working in her daughter's school as a volunteer, hearing children read on a Thursday afternoon, when her younger child was at pre-school. Part-way through the year, the school received some additional funding to support a child with SEMH needs for two hours a day. It was suggested that Laura applied for the job, which she got.

This child then moved on to a specialist placement and Laura's contract ended. But she liked working in school, so applied for a role as a midday supervisor. During the year

> there was a vacancy for a part-time role in one of the classes, so Laura took this on as well.
>
> The following September, once both Laura's children were in school, she began a role as a full-time classroom TA, which she loved, but after 18 months she wanted a new challenge. She completed an Elkan course and became the school's specialist TA for language and communication.
>
> However, soon after she started this role, the head identified that Laura had worked as a counsellor and suggested she did ELSA (emotional literacy support assistant) training. She completed this training and moved into that role, but at the same time decided to reduce her hours to give her more time to support her own children.
>
> Within four years, Laura had moved from being a part-time volunteer through six full- and part-time roles in the school.

This kind of career path, dependent on roles as they come up, staff's interests, prior qualifications or experiences, and moving between full- and part-time roles, is common for many TAs.

The vast number of roles undertaken by TAs adds to the confusion about what their job actually is. It also makes it hard for members of the senior leadership team (SLT), teachers or TAs themselves to know what a TA should be doing and whether they are doing it well.

Challenge 4: Confusion between a teacher and a TA

In many schools, the children and parents make little real distinction between the teacher and the TA, particularly when TAs take on direct teaching roles.

While in most classes, the teacher takes the lead with planning and identifying roles for the TA(s), some TAs work largely or at least partly independently in pedagogical roles: planning for intervention groups, providing cover for absence and PPA times, and occasionally leading classes. Many are responsible for differentiating learning for some of the most vulnerable children, with SEND and other needs.

> ### Case study
>
> Lola is a native Spanish speaker and working as a TA in a small primary school. For many years, the school taught French as their modern foreign language. However, the staff's poor French language skills meant that this became increasingly unsuccessful. It was decided that the school would change to teaching Spanish and ask Lola to deliver this. She was released from her classroom duties for part of the week to plan the Spanish lessons, which she then delivered across the school.

In this case, it would be hard to tell the difference between Lola and a teacher. She planned and delivered her own lessons, following her own curriculum plans, and assessed the children's progress. To a greater or lesser extent, this is the experience of many TAs. However, TAs are not teachers, and few can or should be expected to work alone as Lola did.

The confusion about TAs' roles in the classroom has led to a concern that TAs are being used as cheap cover and are even replacing teachers. Given that TAs lack the professional qualifications of teachers and are paid less, this is an unsurprising consequence of their taking on teaching roles. This can be a challenge in itself, as frequently TAs are asked to deliver lessons, often without any opportunity to prepare, yet they are held to the same standards as teachers. As the TAs cannot support themselves and are rarely replaced when they become the primary deliverer of teaching, they regularly find themselves delivering lessons with less support than the teachers whom they are replacing.

The confusion about when TAs are acting as 'teachers' and when they are not often exacerbates any difficulties in TA–teacher relationships. Neither is sure where their roles begin and end. When things are going well, this can be worked out. When things are going less smoothly, the result can be jealousy and a lack of trust between the adults working in the classroom.

Challenge 5: Lack of job security

There is a significant underlying difference in the form and level of scrutiny faced by teachers and TAs, which impacts on the way they work with each other. The inspection of teachers through Ofsted focuses on how they should do their jobs better, improve outcomes and drive up standards, while the focus for TAs has been on whether their jobs should even exist. The work of the Maximising the Impact of Teaching Assistants (MITA) project and others translated into headlines suggesting that rather than supporting the learning of the children they worked with, TAs were inhibiting it.

Added to this is the threat that in a time of budget cuts a school could run without TAs. Their jobs are constantly being evaluated, particularly for those on short-term contracts or who have contracts tied to specific SEND children. This leaves many TAs feeling insecure, threatened and defensive.

> 'The rules on being a TA in my school can change like the weather: One day you are the teacher when there is a staff shortage (and no, we don't get extra pay), next you will be expected to be whatever the school wants you to be.'
>
> TA

There is an additional level of job insecurity, as many TAs are frequently moved between different roles as staffing and children's needs change. This can be mid-year, at short notice and with little or no consultation. This means that TAs are constantly trying to renegotiate their relationships with children and teachers. This can reduce their willingness and commitment to engage in the school, diminishing their effectiveness.

Challenge 6: Who becomes a TA and why?

In most schools, there will be a huge range of experience within the TA workforce, from those with little or no post-16 education to those with degrees and a number with teaching or other specialist qualifications. They also cover the full age range, from those gaining work experience before going to university to those who are past retirement age. The reality is that the majority of TAs are female, with low pay and perceived low status (Cozens, 2014).

Many TAs are parents who are keen to save on the childcare costs and hassle involved in working during the school holidays. Although many stay in the role after their children leave the school and are deeply committed to it, this demographic can impact TAs' approach to the role and limit their ability to work beyond school hours.

However, as noted above, TAs have increasingly taken on teaching and other paraprofessional responsibilities – a development not reflected in their pay or conditions, or in the respect given to the role.

Challenge 7: A lack of training

In 2016, there were proposals for the introduction of TA standards to sit alongside the Teachers' Standards (UNISON et al., 2016). However, despite the agreement of the major TA and teaching unions, these were never implemented. A lack of government will and commitment meant that this opportunity to place the role of TAs in schools on a clear and consistent footing was missed.

The issue is exacerbated by the fact that, despite many research recommendations, there is little formal training for TAs. As a result, TAs' professional role and status remain unclear, with no single or uniform career path, consistent system of qualifications or even requirements for appraisal and career or professional development. Many local authorities and some academy trusts run TA training courses, and there is a wide variety of Level 2 and 3 certificates and diplomas aimed at training TAs available both on- and offline. However, the content and focus of these courses are inconsistent.

This leads to uncertainty and ambiguity about TAs' roles and levels of training, even within the same school.

Case study

In one school, there are three levels of TAs employed. Their roles are described as:

- Level 1 or 2: This is a general classroom TA or one-to-one TA. Within this, they help with the running of the room, put up displays, do photocopying, etc. They run small groups and interventions. They undertake break and lunch duties. Many are trained to deliver first aid. They benchmark reading and take out students with reasonable adjustments (Equality and Human Rights Commission, 2015) for their assessments. They supervise and support during school trips, parents' evenings and after-school clubs.
- Level 3: These TAs do all the above plus covering classes for PPA or illness. They might run their own small classes or groups on a regular basis.

Further, there is no clear demarcation between TAs and HLTAs (higher level teaching assistants) or different forms of HLTA roles. The distinction between them may be related to their qualifications, to the completion of a specialist course or simply to the responsibilities undertaken. Many staff have mixed roles and are paid at one level when they undertake a TA role and another when they undertake a 'higher–level' role, e.g. absence cover or leading the breakfast club.

Often TAs start their role when there is a need to employ someone to support a particular child or in a particular class. In many parts of the country, recruiting TAs is not easy, so finding someone with the right 'attitude' often overrides concerns about qualifications or experience.

Further, school budgets are tight so training is rarely a priority and training for TAs even less so. Moreover, much of schools' in-house training is focused on INSET days, but many TAs' contracts don't include the requirement to attend all INSET days, so they often miss out on these training opportunities.

Even worse, all too often when they are on site for INSET days, TAs are put on 'tidying duties' rather than actually being offered training. Their training is often limited to statutory elements such as safeguarding and first aid, not pedagogy. When pedagogical training is offered, it tends to be focused on developing understanding about specific forms of special needs or delivering specific interventions. This ignores TAs' wider learning support roles and the need to develop their skills around them. As a result, TAs' training is often based on insecure foundations, as they are taught higher level skills but without the opportunity to develop a basic understanding of how children learn and how best to support and promote this.

```
        Lack of clarity
        about the role
       ↗              ↘
Staff not properly      No clear training
trained to do the  ←    to do the role
      role
```

At the root of the TA training issue is school leaders' uncertainty about what they want their TAs to do: if you don't know what TAs are for, you will be unclear about what training to provide for them. This sets up a vicious circle of minimal or inappropriate training, exacerbating the lack of clarity about expectations or roles, leading to training that is inadequate to support TAs' career development or simply to enable them to do their job better.

Challenge 8: Issues of time

A key difficulty with the establishment and development of the working relationship, never mind any kind of friendship, between teachers and TAs is the issue of time. TA contracts tend to be for the school day only – just the time that children are on site. At best they may be lucky enough to have 15 minutes or even half an hour at one or other end of the day to liaise with their teacher.

Despite over a decade of research demonstrating the importance of teachers and TAs sharing planning and liaison time, this is too often seen as a luxury beyond the reach of the school budget. So schools tend to rely on goodwill and the relationship between teacher and TA for the sharing of planning and information about children.

> 'My LA (learning assistant) and I constantly share ideas and discuss progress and next steps or challenges. Normally over lunch!'
>
> Teacher

If you ask your TAs to give up their time for liaison, you need to remember that many TAs are very poorly paid, often not paid for breaks and only entitled to 30 minutes or less for lunch. To ask them to give more and stay on for even a few extra minutes is a tall order.

Case study

Mandy and her TA, Fiona, were best friends. They had worked together for years. When Mandy was promoted to the SLT,

> Fiona was delighted for her friend and pleased by the idea that she would be paid as an HLTA to provide Mandy with a morning's leadership time once a fortnight. However, both underestimated how much time Mandy would have to spend dealing with 'things' outside of the classroom, often leaving Fiona to have to manage the class at no notice. On top of this, Mandy was frequently delayed returning to the classroom after breaks as she was called to sort out playground incidents.
>
> As the term went on, Fiona became more and more resentful about the time she was expected to spend alone with the class, and about losing her breaks due to Mandy starting lessons late. She felt that she was being expected to take on more duties due to Mandy's increased responsibility, but without any recognition or recompense.
>
> Things came to a head when one of the children commented that Fiona was not as smiley as she used to be. Mandy heard and questioned this. Luckily, their long-standing relationship meant that Mandy and Fiona were able to work it out, so that Fiona's breaks were protected and there were times when Mandy reminded other senior leaders that she had a class and couldn't sort things out straight away.

We need to respect TAs' breaks and make sure that they have time to do the basics like go to the toilet or get a drink. Too often an incident on the playground, an upset child or a teacher, or a request from a member of SLT to 'just do x' eats into TAs' breaks. We can all live with this occasionally, but we must beware of any erosion of a TA's right to breaks and ensure that they are not made to feel guilty for taking them or pressurised into staying after their hours.

However, the lack of liaison time means that many TAs are working on the wing, making it up as they go along and learning the information they are expected to teach at the same time as the children. Few of us do our best work under these conditions. Most of our TAs know this and so give additional time voluntarily. It is vital that we acknowledge this and don't take it for granted.

Challenge 9: Questions of preparedness, deployment and practice

Even though individually they remain poorly paid, TAs' pay forms a significant element in most school budgets – in 2020 about 15 per cent of a primary school budget (Education Policy Institute, 2020). Further, TAs have been seen as the answer to the problems of inclusion and the need to drive up standards. This means that their role has been under constant scrutiny as it has developed. Much of this work has been under the auspices of what has become known as the MITA (Maximising the Impact of Teaching Assistants) project, which is increasingly closely linked with the EEF (Education Endowment Foundation).

The MITA work began in 2003 with the DISS – the Deployment and Impact of Support Staff study – and continues to publish research in this field. Their landmark study in 2013 questioned the impact of TAs on children's learning, finding that while teachers found TAs supportive, they made little difference to children's attainment and at times hampered it. Indeed, often the more support children had, the less progress they made. However, their 2021 work focused on primary schools and the project recognised the value of TAs, describing them as 'the mortar in the brickwork: they hold schools together in numerous and sometimes unnoticed ways' (Webster et al., 2021, p. 2). At the same time, there was a recognition that, like mortar, TAs operate in the gaps, so there is a lack of clarity about their roles and much of their importance is hidden.

The ongoing research has identified the three key issues in TA deployment as:

- preparedness
- deployment
- practice.

This is described in the Wider Pedagogical Role model (WPR). It places the responsibility for these issues at the door of school leaders, beyond the class teacher's control and caused by decisions that were little to do with TAs themselves. It argues that only by acting on working hours and staff training can school leaders increase the effectiveness of teaching assistants as a group.

The ongoing work from MITA, the EEF and others has changed much of the thinking about how TAs are deployed. However, the issues of a lack of time for liaison between teachers and TAs, and a lack of clarity about TAs' roles and their training, remain.

Challenge 10: Using TAs to promote inclusion?

Since the Warnock Report (1978), there has been an ongoing debate on the meaning of inclusion, including the role of the TA in promoting inclusion. Often a TA is seen as 'the answer' for children with SEND and the default response to a child with an EHCP. However, much of this support can become focused on accessing learning (often at a piece-by-piece level), and issues of inclusion across the curriculum and wider school life are lost. TAs can find themselves focusing on task completion, rather than developing children's skills to access learning with increased independence. Children with SEND often spend much of their time in intervention groups or seated separately within the classroom – often to the back or side of the room. This can mean that their learning is effectively outsourced to a TA, who becomes their primary educator in place of the teacher. This can become exclusion or segregation masquerading as inclusion.

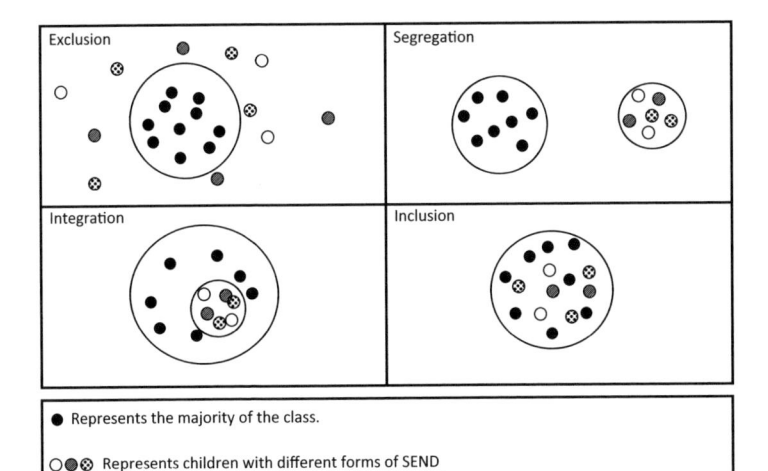

Exclusion	Segregation
Integration	Inclusion

● Represents the majority of the class.
○ ● ⊗ Represents children with different forms of SEND

This is exacerbated when the model of TA deployment in schools is based, as it often is, on 'what we have always done', rather than on considering the needs of the children in a particular cohort or on developing our understanding of inclusion. This is hard to challenge, particularly for new staff.

The final challenge!

The next step is for all teachers to be able to take a proactive role in developing effective working relationships with their TA(s), so that together they can support and promote children's learning, wellbeing and inclusion. To do this, this book will look at:

- making TA deployment work in your classroom
- working together effectively to support children with SEND
- effective relationships to support children's learning
- strategies to support and promote learning

- making the best use of your TA throughout the lesson
- using interventions to support learning, and TAs' role in this
- sharing information, including planning and feedback, with your TA
- working with your TAs to support behaviour.

1 Understanding what you want your TA to do in the classroom

'I think the most important thing is matching the TA to their specific role. It isn't as simple as one TA can do any TA role well. Each TA brings something specific to the school.'

TA

Most schools have guidelines about the physical environment of your classroom; however, much of the control over it is in your hands. Similarly, while you have little direct control over who the other adults in your classroom are, and while there are rules about how you work with and deploy them, you have considerable discretion as to who does what and how in your classroom.

To take full advantage of your freedom to shape how you and your TA work together may require real diplomatic skill, particularly if you want to change the way a TA works. It needs partnership with the TA and is easier with the support of the school's senior leaders.

Who's who in the classroom

Key to working out what you want your TA to do is understanding their role, particularly given the variety of different job titles used in different schools.

TA roles fit roughly into four main types, though TAs often undertake more than one role.

1. 'General' TA

A general class TA is usually funded from a range of sources, including the main school budget, SEND support and PP (pupil premium) funding. Often there is a standard allocation of TA support given to a class regardless of the children's specific needs. General TA support is usually weighted towards literacy and numeracy lessons, the younger year groups and Year 6.

Their role in the classroom is, generally, to support learning and the teacher as the teacher sees fit for educational and practical tasks. General TAs may provide support for those with SEND, EAL (English as an additional language), PP, etc. Often, they will set up and organise resources, listen to pupils reading and carry out assessments like spelling tests in the classroom. In many cases, they will have additional roles outside the classroom, such as playground duties, first aid, admin tasks and emotional and pastoral support.

2. Specialists providing specific provisions and interventions outside the classroom

Increasingly, all TAs are expected to lead intervention groups of different kinds, so this has become part of the role of the general TA. Over and above this, some TAs with additional training and/or specific qualifications will lead specialist interventions related to academic needs, support for children with specific special needs or SEMH needs. The increased focus on mental health issues and phonics has led to a growth in these roles. We will look at interventions in more detail in Chapter 6.

3. Targeted support for special needs within the classroom

Much of the recent increase in the number of TAs is related to SEND support, including EHCPs. Some staff are employed to work with particular children and may even have them named in their contract.

This will affect, though not necessarily to the extent that you expect, what a TA is willing and able to do in the classroom.

> **EXTRA USEFUL INFORMATION: Funding streams for vulnerable groups**
>
> Different TA roles are financed by specific funding streams, beyond the main school budget, including:
>
> - SEND funding, which is divided into the notional SEND budget (related to the number of children with SEND in the school) and funding related to specific children with EHCPs
> - funding related to particular cohorts of pupils, e.g. pupil premium, the children of serving military families, looked-after children, etc.
> - specific grants, e.g. the PE and sport premium.
>
> It is not always easy to identify the funding source for a particular role in a school and some roles are funded by multiple sources. However, the source of the funding for a TA's role will influence what they do in school. For example, EHCP funding should provide support for the child with the EHCP and there should be a benefit to pupil premium pupils from pupil premium funding.

4. Early Years support

According to the EYFS framework (DfE, 2021), the staff-to-pupil ratio for nursery classes and in nursery schools is at least one staff member – at least one of whom must be a qualified teacher – for every 13 children. For Reception classes, the staff ratio is 30 children per schoolteacher; however, there is often at least one additional adult in a Reception class. This supports the 'key person' approach, which is statutory throughout the Early Years, including in Reception classes (though this looks different in a Reception class compared to a nursery, due to the different adult-to-child ratio).

Yet the principle remains the same. *'The key person helps a child feel confident that they are "held in mind", thought about and loved'* (Early Years Coalition, 2021, p. 30). They build and maintain a relationship with each child and their family. The teacher needs to retain an overview of all the children in their class but benefits from the key person's specific knowledge about and relationships with each child, which supports a sense of shared responsibility and teamwork across the setting.

Appreciating what your TA does

Even within these different roles, there are a wide range of tasks TAs are asked to carry out. These commonly divide into:

- pedagogical (teaching) tasks
- non-pedagogical (everything else) tasks.

The situation is complicated, as often staff perform more than one role, often combining teaching and non-teaching elements. For example, a TA employed to support a child with an EHCP could be responsible for supporting their physical or emotional needs (non-pedagogical), but usually will support their learning needs (pedagogical) as well.

Case study

Maeve has cerebral palsy and is a wheelchair user. She needs support from a TA to transfer between her outdoor and her indoor chairs, to transfer to and from her standing frame, for her OT and physio exercises and for intimate care – all non-pedagogical tasks. Additionally, Maeve has learning difficulties. In Year 5, despite a range of strategies, she is still working within the Year 1 curriculum, so she also needs significant pedagogical support.

Although promoting inclusion requires all staff to engage with all elements of the role, not all TAs are confident or able to do this. This may affect how they see themselves and respond to the expectations placed on them.

Case study

Maureen had started work at the school in 1995 as a dinner lady, when her children were small. Over the years, she started doing more in the classrooms – hearing children read, helping with art and craft projects, putting up displays, etc. Over more years, she supported children with SEND and helped as a general class TA.

By 2015, Maureen was working entirely in the classroom. She was increasingly being asked to lead intervention groups and support children with maths and literacy. Maureen had not done well at school and lacked the skills and confidence to do this effectively. Having worked happily and effectively in the school for many years, she was now failing because the role and expectations had changed.

It is very hard for staff, like Maureen, employed to do one thing, but in a changing world expected to do another. It is also difficult if you are asked to work with a TA who lacks the skills the job requires. Unfortunately, it often falls to you to support staff in these situations, though help should be available and sought from others.

If this isn't working…	…try this
Lena, a TA, worked to support George who had difficulties with speech, language and literacy. The speech and language therapist had recommended using Colourful Semantics (Carter and Coleman, 2020) to support his understanding of sentence structure. Lena was given a pack of Colourful Semantics resources. She took them home, went through them and watched the training video. She came into school the next day and photocopied and laminated what she thought she needed. She understood how this was supposed to work for the topics in the pack, but not how it was supposed to relate to what they were doing in the classroom. For the next few weeks, Lena muddled through and did her best. However, when the speech and language therapist returned, she complained that the intervention wasn't being used properly.	When Lena was given the pack recommended by the speech and language therapist, the SENCo sat her down and went through it. She modelled how to use the examples in the pack and explained that these were only examples. The SENCo and class teacher looked at the planning for the following week. Then the SENCo worked with Lena to identify ways Colourful Semantics could be used in the classroom for that topic. They identified key vocabulary and the appropriate resources, so that George could use them to build simple sentences. The SENCo also organised a training session for Lena, her class teacher and some other staff using this approach, which allowed the more experienced staff to share tips and resources.

Understanding who is in your classroom and why

There are a range of factors that influence who is deployed to work in your class. Most are unfortunately beyond your control and often beyond the control of your school's senior leaders, who must keep within budget while complying with employment law and a wide range of other legislation, statutory and non-statutory guidance.

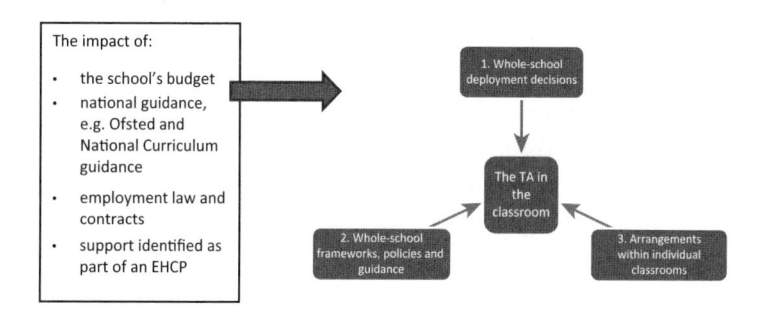

The impact of:
- the school's budget
- national guidance, e.g. Ofsted and National Curriculum guidance
- employment law and contracts
- support identified as part of an EHCP

→ The TA in the classroom
1. Whole-school deployment decisions
2. Whole-school frameworks, policies and guidance
3. Arrangements within individual classrooms

1. Whole-school deployment decisions

The senior leaders' deployment decisions are immensely complex and based on a wide variety of strategic, financial and personnel factors. This means neither you nor your TA have much influence over:

- the level of TA support in your classroom
- who the individual TAs are
- how long they are there for
- what duties they are expected to undertake outside of the classroom
- whether support is provided by a single person or split between two or more people.

> **Personal story**
>
> *When I was a head of inclusion in a large primary school with an attached nursery and Children's Centre, a speech and language unit and a nurture group, I was responsible for the deployment of about 50 full- and part-time support staff. It was a nightmare. I used to start with a list of all the children with SEND and their hours and levels of need, which were sorted into classes and year groups and had all the staff's names on sticky notes with their working hours. Then I had a table showing the classes and days of the week and the information about staff preferences for where they wanted to work. I had to try to solve the puzzle, so that all the children had the support they needed and as many staff as possible were working where they wanted.*
>
> *It used to take days. Every time I took a draft to the rest of the SLT, they would point out that 'so and so' didn't work on Tuesdays, that Mel hated such and such a teacher or even that I had missed out someone entirely or that someone else was needed to run a particular intervention and couldn't be in two places simultaneously. Then I would return to the drawing board and try again.*

It is always worth discussing whole-school deployment decisions with senior leaders in your school; however, there may be issues and implications that can be difficult to see when you are focused on your own class. They may not be able to discuss all these issues with you.

2. Whole-school frameworks, policies and guidance

Most schools have guidance about how TAs are deployed within the classroom, for example:

- their use for interventions, to cover absence or PPA
- whether TAs can be moved from class to class
- whether they follow the child or the subject
- whether they are allowed or expected to have their own working space within the classroom
- expectations about how they should hear children read or support maths
- their liaison with the SENCo.

This is recorded in different places in different schools and is not always easy to find. It might be in the staff handbook, or the teaching and learning, SEND or TA policies. Nevertheless, this guidance should form the basis for how you work with your TA(s). It is worth looking at with your TA; sometimes, TAs will see what they did with their last teacher as the norm across the school, even though it differs from the school policy.

3. Arrangements within individual classrooms

It is only once you have dealt with the external issues that you can begin to personalise and directly influence how you work with the TAs in your own classroom. The following sections in this chapter explain how you can begin this.

Establishing roles

As part of the process of shaping how you and your TA work together, you need to know who they are and understand their skills, experience and role. Even more importantly, you need to consider the needs of your class. Even if you have a brilliant handover with the previous teacher, it is not always possible to know or understand a class's needs before you start working with them. Also, as the children change, mature and develop, their needs change. Additionally, mobility (if children move schools mid-year) can change the class's needs and dynamics.

If this isn't working…	…try this
Lucie was always super organised. She started the school year with lists and timetables for how she and her TAs were going to work together, who would be the key person for which children and which interventions would run when. She arranged times to go through this and how she would share the planning with each of the TAs individually. She listened to their ideas and incorporated them into the plans and reshared them.	Lucie used her various lists and plans for general classroom organisation. But four weeks into term, she met with her TAs and reviewed the interventions. She found that some children were making great progress and needed either different or no interventions. There were a couple of children, including a child who had arrived two weeks into term, who needed more support. She changed the interventions. She also swapped the staff, as she discovered one person was much stronger in maths than literacy.
The first half term went remarkably smoothly, everything was in its place and the children were making good progress. Lucie breathed a huge sigh of relief and felt that she could do this.	Again, at half term, Lucie arranged a time to sit down and review what was happening. It was really useful to have the TAs' perspectives. One of them had heard from a few parents about concerns with homework.
But by mid-November, there were signs that not all was right. Several children were becoming disruptive, and their progress was stalling. A group of parents were asking awkward questions about homework. Lucie began to question herself and started having migraines.	By reviewing and changing, rather than regarding her systems as set in stone, Lucie was able to work more successfully with both the children and the TAs.

Having a plan for how you and your TA(s) will work together is an important starting point. But to be effective, this needs to be a working document that is adapted and adjusted as the year goes on. Ideally, both you and your TA(s) will be able to share ideas and contribute to this plan.

Working relationships

Making the teacher/TA relationship work is about the willingness to listen and learn. All relationships take time to develop and have ups and downs. It is reasonable and to be expected that there may be points of tension between you and your TA. Hopefully, they are short-lived and few and far between, but they are normal. Both parties may be affected by stresses and anxieties in other parts of their lives, which may impact on relationships in the classroom. TAs want teachers to share the load so that they can be supportive. Equally, they want to be treated as equals and not as a dogsbody or slave.

Many teachers and TAs speak about the importance of working together, and of friendships established in the classroom lasting many years. Indeed, so many teachers and TAs do form close bonds that it is easy to assume that this is how it should be. In truth, this is a working relationship. It needs to be effective to support children and their learning – any friendship is a bonus!

Sharing the role

A lack of time means that not only are TAs often on the back foot with learning content, but also there is little or no time to share or consider their role within the lesson. This means that often the roles established early in your teacher/ TA relationship become set in stone and difficult to change or adapt. This can be a particular problem for early career teachers (ECTs), who want to make changes as their practice and knowledge of their class develops.

As a new teacher, you may be very dependent on your TA's knowledge and understanding of the school and how it works, particularly if they are a long-established member of staff. Their expertise about how the photocopier works, where the coffee is kept, children's family histories and how children were supported previously can be invaluable. But it can also be overwhelming, making it difficult to establish ownership of the class without creating conflict – a silent or not-so-silent battle about how best to manage and support learning in the classroom.

If this isn't working...	...try this
Gina had a clear set of strategies she wanted to use with her class to support their maths. She was a firm believer in using apparatus and concrete resources to support children and promote their understanding. Anna, her TA, felt that these resources were lots of bits that fell on the floor and got in the way. Their lack of agreement meant these resources were used inconsistently and it was confusing for the children.	Gina realised she had assumed that because it was obvious to her how the concrete resources helped learning, it must be obvious to Anna too. After all, Anna was in the room when Gina modelled their use to the children. However, she had never explained the reasons for their use to Anna, because she assumed that Anna would understand it implicitly. So, Gina arranged cover so that she and Anna could sit down and go through the resources, discuss how they worked and why she was using them. Once Anna understood this, she was much happier and more confident to use them.

'Mind reading' is not part of the training for teachers or TAs. It is easy for us to assume that the reasons for using particular approaches or strategies in the classroom, often based on our training and professional understanding, will be clear to others. However, TAs do not receive the same training or enjoy the same professional experience. The difficulty can be to identify what the TA doesn't know and then to find the time to explain it. This is exacerbated as neither teachers nor TA are trained on how to work together.

If this isn't working...	...try this
Zuza was increasingly struggling to manage her class. Every time she gave instructions to the class, her TA, Jasminder, repeated them, changing them slightly. Zuza tried talking to Jasminder and sought the support of the SLT, but with little impact. Jasminder continued to undermine her and disrupt the learning.	Zuza decided to change tack and asked Jasminder about how she saw her role and what she saw as her job. Jasminder explained that she was supporting the children by making sure that they knew what to do. Zuza then asked if Jasminder could do this by recording a written list of the instructions (with added visuals where possible) as a prompt for the children rather than verbally repeating them. Jasminder was delighted; she knew that she was being useful and had a clear role. This reduced the confusion of repeated instructions, and the written instructions provided better support for learning.

Despite research emphasising the importance of training and finding time to communicate, this remains a low priority in many schools. This means that creating time for communication, which may prevent the breakdown of a relationship, often depends on the staff's positive relationships. This can create a vicious circle, when communication is not good and the time needed to alleviate this issue is dependent on a relationship made more difficult due to poor communication. In these situations, it is important that staff are open and honest and, if necessary, seek support from senior colleagues.

Feeling valued and respected

Difficulties can happen when we don't make TAs feel valued and part of the team. Despite their often vast experience and knowledge, TAs still can feel quite insecure. They want teachers to ask their opinions and share feedback and they want to know that this is valued. Too often praise for success in the classroom goes to the teacher and not the TA. In the hustle and bustle of the classroom, it is easy to forget to let your TA know what they have done well. You can find yourselves in a situation where you only pick up on what your TA has done wrong and assume that they know when things are going well. A simple thank you goes a long way.

Case study

Suzette was a new TA. She had been taken on as a TA in Year 6 to cover a maternity leave, so had joined the class mid-year. She was placed in the class with little experience of schools beyond her own school years and that of her children. Pressures of time meant that Suzette was expected to pick up from where her colleague had left off and slot into what was happening in the classroom. The teacher tried to 'grab' the odd moment to explain, but it was all a bit hit and miss.

As the weeks went on, Suzette learned fast and became more confident and adept at understanding what she needed to do. Everyone in the class seemed so busy. She listened carefully in lessons, watched what the teacher and the other TA were doing, read the children's individual support plans in the evenings and sent the SENCo emails to ask about strategies and approaches. But she had no way of knowing whether she was getting it right.

It was only after the deputy head caught her having a quick cry in the toilets that everyone realised that in their rush and focus on the children, no one had given Suzette a proper explanation of her role or told her how well she was doing.

At the same time, we need to ensure that our thanks and praise for our TAs are genuine and respectful of their professionalism. Many TAs complain of being patronised and praised like the children. It can be a difficult balance to achieve and one we need to be aware of and give thought to. However, remembering to say thank you is basic in a successful working relationship.

Respecting their knowledge

Our TAs bring to the classroom skills, experience and knowledge, often in areas we lack. Often, they spend longer with individual children than we can – not just sitting beside them as they learn but also out on the playground – so our TAs may know the children and what motivates them better than we do. We are responsible for the whole class, while our TAs are more able to focus on individuals and small groups. This can give them invaluable insights into the children and their world. We need them to share this, so it can feed into how we support the children.

Further, many TAs are embedded (and live) within the local community in a way that fewer teachers are. This means TAs can often bring their knowledge of the local community, the lives of the children beyond the school gates and the interrelationships within the community into the classroom. In many schools, knowing who is whose cousin is vital information that does not appear on any school record, but may have a key influence on your seating plan.

As with so many things, in teacher/TA relationships the difficulty is sharing this knowledge. Too often a TA will assume that teachers know what they know. Equally, there can be times when it feels as if your TA is trying to use their knowledge to take over.

Case study

Rita entered teaching in her early forties after having children and a successful career in business. Her TA, Kate, had worked in the school for more than ten years. She had always been in Year 5 and had clear views on how things should be done. It was expected that Kate would be supportive to Rita as she settled into her new role and the school. This was true, provided that Rita didn't wish to change anything from how it had always been done. However, Rita did want to change things. This led to huge conflicts and tensions, making both Rita and Kate very unhappy.

It took considerable mediation and support from various members of the SLT for Kate and Rita to work through their difficulties.

Ten years later, they are still working together, largely using Rita's ideas, but with regular input from Kate. Kate can always be counted on to give a different point of view and make Rita think through what she is doing and why.

Playing to their strengths

The art is to understand and use TAs' strengths by giving them opportunities and space to use their initiative. TA and teacher relationships are most successful when they enable both parties to 'play to their strengths'.

> 'We pay TAs far less than they deserve for the work they do and one way to make the job more rewarding is to ensure they are able to use their skills and strengths – it's just dumb not to. But some schools are dumb!'
>
> SENCo

In some cases, this involves the TA taking the lead in specific parts of the curriculum or school day. I know that, as a teacher, I was always very grateful for a musical TA who would deliver at least part of the music curriculum with me, or even for me, to make up for my complete lack of musical ability.

> ### Case study
>
> Chloe is a Year 2 teacher. She slipped and fell on some ice and broke her ankle. With the support of her TA, Amy, and a willing band of children who were eager to help, Chloe just about managed in school balanced on her crutches. However, teaching PE was a step too far. It was only at this point that Amy revealed that she had always loved PE and still played netball most weeks.
>
> A quick bit of reorganisation meant that Chloe could plan the PE lessons and Amy deliver them (under Chloe's supervision).
>
> It quickly became clear that this was an area where Amy had natural talent and enthusiasm while Chloe understood the process of learning but had no great love for PE.
>
> Even after Chloe's ankle had healed, allowing Amy to take the lead in PE lessons meant that Amy could share her enthusiasm, and the children were more engaged and learned better. Meanwhile Chloe took on the 'TA' role and supported those who, like herself, struggled with the physical coordination required for PE. This gave her an opportunity to observe the children and experience a different kind of relationship with them, which improved her teaching in other areas.

While your TA should work under your direction, there are areas where it may be appropriate for you and your TA to 'swap roles' so they take the lead. This approach allows you time to observe and work with individuals. At the same time, it ensures that your TA feels valued, and is able to share and develop their skills. For the children, this gives them access to someone with a different skill set and allows them to see that this is valued.

In order to work, this kind of role swapping requires honesty and effective communication. TAs can be frustrated by watching their teacher deliver something that they feel they could do a better job of delivering. Equally, teachers can be frustrated when their TA 'takes over' a lesson or offers views and engages in what the teacher feels to be an inappropriate manner.

If this isn't working...	...try this
Sol was an ECT and just gaining his confidence. At times, he was aware that he paused to gather his thoughts and think how best to express his ideas. Bano, his TA, wanted to help and often jumped in to supply the word or idea that she thought he was searching for. This made it more difficult for Sol to think of what he wanted to say. He could feel that he was getting more and more irritated with Bano, which was spoiling their relationship. This was beginning to impact on the children as he snapped at her.	Sol decided to talk to his mentor about how to manage this. He understood that Bano was trying to help. Following his mentor's advice, Sol shared with his class that sometimes he needed to pause and think through ideas before he could express them clearly. He talked about the importance of taking 'thinking time' to sort your ideas out. After this, Bano jumped in less and the children began to talk about taking thinking time, which improved their learning.

Making it work

All the children should be able to access time and attention from their class teacher. It is very easy for the lowest achieving children or those with special needs to become 'sidelined' to the care of your TA, who becomes their main educator. TAs can end up always working with these groups, particularly if the funding for their role comes from sources aimed at supporting the groups. This can become a form of exclusion.

> ### Case study
>
> Bryony had autism and struggled with change. She felt safe and comfortable with Lottie, the class TA. Without Lottie's supportive presence, Bryony could be very disruptive. She fidgeted in her chair, chewed bits of paper, including her exercise books, and made random noises. She got little or no work done.
>
> Over the year, it became easier for Lottie to sit with Bryony during lessons. Lottie became her go-to person when things went wrong. It was only when Julia, her teacher, came to review her SEND support plan and write her end-of-year report that she realised how little she knew about Bryony and her learning. The reality was that Julia had rarely worked with Bryony because Lottie was always with her. Bryony had been effectively excluded from Julia's class.

There are many ways of ensuring that all children access teacher time and are not taught exclusively by a TA. These include:

- <u>Rotating through the week</u>

  Most classes are organised in some way into groups that work together or at least on the same task at the same time. Often the teacher and TA(s) will work with the same groups each day or for a few days at a time. By rotating through the week, you can ensure that both you and any TAs work with each group at some point during the week.

  It is important to ensure not only that you work with each group, but that, over time, you work with each group at different times of the week and stages in the learning process. It is easy to organise things so that you always work with a particular group on a Monday and another group on a Tuesday and so on, but too often this means that you are always with one group for drafting and another for editing, meaning their teacher support is focused on a single part of the learning process.

- Flipping the roles
  Often your TA sits with a group while you undertake the 'roving'/'triaging' role: answering children's questions, picking up and challenging misconceptions and marking work as you go. Instead of your TA staying still and you moving, this pattern can be reversed so that you are able to give focused attention to a group while your TA does the problem-solving and class management.

- The 'cut away' concept[2]
  Often all the children in a class sit through the whole introduction to a piece of learning. This can mean that children who have already grasped a concept or strategy are listening to something that they already know and understand, while others who lack the foundational learning or key vocabulary to understand the learning are sitting through something that they cannot access.

  In both cases, these children are learning little and can often respond with disruption. The concept of 'cut away' is to reduce the time that children are listening to an input that is not promoting their learning. There are various models of doing this, which include:

Model 1	Model 2
• All the children start together, engaging in the teacher input.	• A 'less able' group starts with the TA on a reinforcement or recap task.
• A 'more able' group is sent off to start the task.	• The teacher introduces the new learning to the remainder of the class.
• The remainder of the class continue to engage with the explanation and worked examples.	• They then start the task and independent working. The TA moves to these groups.
• The remainder of the class start independent working.	• The teacher then works on the new learning with the 'less able' group.
• The teacher works with the 'more able' group, supporting them with an extension task.	

[2] This is developed from the work completed by Dr Keith Watson for NACE.

Model 3	Model 4
• The whole class starts together. • During the input, the teacher regularly stops for self-evaluation. As children feel confident, they move to independent work. • The teacher continues to work directly with those who feel that they need continued input. The TA supports the remaining children. • This needs to be supported by good Assessment for Learning.	• The 'more able' group start on a problem-solving or mastery task. • The 'less able' group start on a reinforcement or recap task, working with the TA. • The teacher works with the majority of the class. Once they are ready for independent work, the teacher moves to the other groups.

In this approach, it is important that the 'more able' and 'less able' groups are not static but reflect children's strengths and difficulties with the day's task. For example, a child who struggles with number work may shine at shape work and vice versa.

- Zoning the room

  In this approach, the room is divided into zones and each adult takes responsibility for the support of the children in an area of the room. This reduces the number of children that adults are trying to observe and work with. It avoids all the adults becoming clustered around one group of children while others are left to flounder.

Conclusion

TA deployment remains one of the most difficult issues for the classroom teacher, as so much of it is tied up with issues beyond your control. You are unlikely to be able to influence the hours your TAs works, which impacts on your ability to share information and planning or even to form a relationship with them. Your focus should be on what you can control. You need to think about how to deploy your TA so that all the children receive quality time with you, as well as effective support from the TA, as part of promoting inclusion and enabling all the children to access learning.

Key points to remember:

- Your role is key to ensuring that all children in your class are supported effectively.
- TAs are funded in different ways and may have different contracts, depending on what they have been employed to do.
- You should not feel that you have failed if you have struggled to communicate effectively when there is not enough time to do so. Instead, you need to explore different ways to achieve this.
- Many TAs choose to go far beyond the expectations and requirements of their contract, but this cannot and should not be taken for granted.
- Don't assume that because a particular set of hours works for you or because long hours are part of the school culture, someone who works different hours is lazy or shirking their responsibilities. The expectations of teachers and TAs vary and different people have different ways of working.

Things to discuss with senior leaders

- What frameworks and guidance exist in your school to support how you and your TA(s) should work together? Are you able to take time to look at these alongside your TA to develop a shared understanding of them?
- What exactly is/are your TA(s) employed to do and how are they funded? You can then reflect this in how you deploy them.

- What information about their role was your TA given as part of their recruitment and induction process? (This will influence their expectations for their role and responses to your direction.)

Things to think about

- Even if you cannot change the culture of your school, what small changes can you undertake in your classroom?
- How can you build an effective working relationship with your TA?
- Does your way of referring to your TA when talking to the children, parents and colleagues promote respect and demonstrate that they are valued? Some TAs do not like to be referred to by teachers as 'my' TA. They are not owned by the teacher and, reasonably, wish to be seen as a valued colleague.

Things that work really well

- It is important to remember what you can and can't do, influence and change about TA deployment in your classroom. It can help to think about this like a 'mindfulness' diagram of what you can and can't control.

Things I can control about TA deployment in my classroom

Things I can't control about TA deployment in my classroom

- Use a 'Classroom Contract' (as discussed on page 198) to identify and record your and your TAs' roles. This should be a working document, which you discuss with them and which you can both change as your relationship develops.
- Try to make time to share planning and learning with your TA. But also remember that time spent in general chat is not wasted. It is part of building a working relationship.
- If you feel that your relationship with your TA is breaking down, do seek help and support from a member of your SLT or a mentor. It is important to take time to talk through the issues, get some perspective and even ask them to support a conversation between you. It is not a failure to take steps to repair a working relationship – the failure would be to do nothing about it.
- It is easier to solve staff deployment issues if you can get the support of senior leaders. It is also easier if you can go to them with a possible solution, rather than a complaint.

2 Focus on support for children with SEND

'When you are supporting a child with SEND, your aim is that they no longer need you.'

TA

Despite the considerable evidence that receiving more TA support can, on occasions, inhibit rather than promote children's learning, the default approach for many children with significant SEND is to offer one-to-one support for some or all of the school day. Many teachers and senior leaders believe that an EHCP indicates that a child needs and is entitled to a one-to-one TA. In fact, only very rarely does an EHCP actually state that a child should receive one-to-one support. Indeed, all the evidence is that this is not what support should look like in a mainstream classroom, except in a very few exceptional cases, where a child has one or more of the following:

- a high level of physical disability or medical needs
- significant developmental needs
- significant safeguarding concerns.

An approach to SEND based solely on one-to-one support for those with the highest level of needs quickly leaves those with less significant needs (SEN Support level) to flounder unsupported – it becomes exclusion presented as inclusion.

Very few adults have another person with them constantly and, providing they are properly supervised, the same should be true for children. The SEND Code of Practice (2015) focuses on preparation for independence and adulthood. Although adulthood seems a long way off for a primary-aged child, we still need to support them to become independent learners, tackle tasks on their own, and experience success and failure. Providing this for all children is a key element of an inclusive environment.

> **EXTRA USEFUL INFORMATION: EHCP funding**
>
> Different local authorities (LAs) write EHCPs in different ways, leading to a high level of confusion and many misconceptions about the provision, hours and funding for EHCPs. The 2022 SEND green paper 'Right support, right place, right time' (DfE, 2022b) includes a promise of uniform digital EHCP and annual review paperwork for the whole country. In the meantime, some LAs list the support in terms of hours, with some information about the provisions and interventions that should be used to support the child. Others give detailed lists of specific interventions, including the time to be spent on them each week. There are many variations in between this, which may include 'top up' or 'high needs funding'.
>
> Where hours or a budget are included on an EHCP, they usually include the hours provided by a £6,000 notional SEND budget. This is generally regarded as funding equivalent to 12 to 13 hours of TA time, so when a child has an ECHP that identifies they should receive 18 hours of support, this is often only five to six hours in addition to their SEN Support funding. This may be reflected in any staffing to support them.

While a TA should work to prompt and support the child's learning, it is vital that the child does not become dependent on the TA. 'The right support at the right time' is the 'holy grail' of supporting children with SEND. It's a tough balancing act: holding off to let the child learn while not letting the child struggle, become disheartened, give up or become disruptive.

> ### Case study
>
> Kian had significant attachment issues, so he was not willing to take any risks with his learning and struggled to attempt any task he felt might be challenging. He had regular and dramatic meltdowns. His hypervigilance meant that he struggled to maintain focus. It was very tempting to provide him with a one-to-one TA who sat with him constantly and supported him through every difficulty. There were times when he needed this very high level of support, but to provide this all the time would have developed prompt-dependence. It was a careful balancing act of providing support to start a task, reducing support once Kian gained confidence, then providing support as he needed it again to help him to maintain focus. By providing the right support at the right time, we enabled Kian to learn and make progress while developing his independence and resilience.

Maximising the child's access to quality teaching

The primary responsibility and oversight of every child's learning must remain with you, and not your TA, and the needs of all children 'must be addressed, first and foremost, through excellent classroom teaching' (Sharples, Webster and Blatchford, 2018). The SEND Code of Practice reminds us:

> 'Teachers are responsible and accountable for the progress and development of the pupils in their class, including where pupils access support from teaching assistants or specialist staff.'
>
> DfE, 2015 p. 99

You need to maximise the learning time all children have with you and ensure their access to quality-first teaching. TAs should be used 'to supplement what teachers do, not replace them' (Sharples et al., 2018, p. 4). However, many children with SEND are regularly taken out of the classroom for intervention groups or sit with a TA for most of the lesson; the TA often becomes the children's primary educator, replacing the teacher. This can become a barrier to their inclusion, particularly if a TA falls back onto the use of closed questions and a focus on task completion. This means when a child begins to struggle, the TA is too quick to supply the answer or correct the child immediately, rather than supporting them to work it out, thus stifling the learning process and independence. Your TA's focus should be to support the child to access the lesson that you are teaching, rather than removing the child to engage in different learning, either in or out of the room.

If this isn't working…	…try this
Otis was in a Year 4 class. He was working within the Year 1 curriculum, so he needed a highly differentiated curriculum. The easiest way to manage this was for his TA to take him out of all literacy and numeracy lessons and work on different activities with him in the corner of the school hall. Otis was not making any progress and many of the activities he took part in were highly repetitive. His class teacher did not know what he was doing as all his learning was planned and delivered by the TA. The TA felt isolated and resentful – after all, she wasn't a teacher but she was working as one for Otis.	It was agreed that Otis should be taught within the classroom, not outside it. As far as possible, he would join in with class inputs. It was quickly found that in English lessons, he could join in discussions about texts that had been read aloud and contribute ideas to other discussions. A peer buddy supported him to develop his ideas. He still needed TA support to record them. In maths, Otis worked on the same area as the rest of the class, but at a lower level. For example, when they did addition of three-digit numbers, he did addition of number bonds to ten. Often the focus of his work could be used as a warm-up with the

whole class. Also, there were other children who benefited from working with Otis on these activities.

The teacher had a much better understanding of what Otis was able to do and so could plan more appropriate and interesting work. The TA was able to swap with the teacher and work with a range of children, so she felt happier, and engaged more effectively with Otis and others. Most importantly, Otis made progress.

Working with your TA to be a helicopter, not Velcro®

How TAs are deployed between classes is fundamentally an SLT issue, but you do have some autonomy about how you use your TA within your classroom. In many schools there is a focus on the 'Velcro®' TA, where a TA constantly works directly with a specific child. However, this approach can lead TAs and teachers to believe that the TA should be with 'their child' only and at all times. It leads to an over reliance on the TA for both the child and the teacher.

An alternative model is the 'helicopter TA'. The helicopter TA prepares the child for learning by 'dropping down' the strategies and resources needed for learning. Then they 'lift off and hover', leaving the child to work independently. They can 'drop down' again when the child needs more support to refocus or to use the strategies and resources available, and then leave again. This approach means that TAs can provide children with both the support they need and opportunities to learn independently. In addition, it can free them to work with other children.

There are advantages and disadvantages to both the Velcro® and helicopter approaches, but in most cases, encouraging your TA to be a 'helicopter' is the best option for them and the child.

Velcro®	Helicopter
In the 'Velcro®' model, the TA is constantly with the child, working directly with them.	In the 'helicopter' model, the TA starts the child off on an activity, then moves away, leaving them to work independently. They work with others. They return to their focus child to: • check in • help with any problems • reassure • refocus. The TA then moves away again, returning as and when they are needed.
Advantages:	Advantages:
✓ There is always someone there when the child needs help. ✓ It is clear that the child has support, which can make them and their parents feel secure. ✓ It is easy to differentiate work to the child's level.	✓ The child can develop independence. ✓ The child learns that they can do things on their own. ✓ The TA can also support others.
Disadvantages:	Disadvantages:
✗ The child becomes dependent on having an adult there to attempt any task. ✗ It undermines the child's and adults' belief that the child can do anything on their own.	✗ We will not always get the timing right, so there is a risk that the child might not have support available at the point at which they need it.

Velcro®	Helicopter
✗ The child becomes dependent on the TA and separated from the teacher. ✗ The child becomes separated from their peers.	

Having a shared understanding of 'classroom support' and inclusion

The 'helicopter' approach requires TAs to be confident and feel that they have permission to leave 'their child'. This requires a shared understanding between TAs, teachers, senior leaders and parents of what is meant by 'classroom support'.

Case study

Rachel was employed to support Karl, who had an EHCP. She and her class teacher had agreed that they would use the helicopter model of working. Rachel loved working with a wider range of children and Karl was becoming increasingly confident and able to work on his own. He was making great progress, particularly in English, where he was now able to record sentences independently, though he needed support with his spelling and punctuation.

However, whenever a senior leader came into the class, Rachel immediately stopped whatever she was doing and scuttled back to Karl's side, disrupting both Karl and those she was working with. Rachel felt that she was employed to work with Karl and therefore she should be working with him all the time, and if she was not, she might be accused of not doing her job properly.

> The deputy head spoke to Rachel and explained that the helicopter approach had been discussed and agreed with Karl's parents at his annual review. This was how she and the SENCo wanted Rachel to work. This gave Rachel the confidence to use this approach fully.

The focus needs to be on supporting a child to access instructions. Rather than concentrating on a child completing a task, the TA needs to focus on how to support their learning using visual reminders and checklists, so the child can attempt the task independently. These resources could include the following:

- <u>Task management boards:</u> These are essentially checklists, breaking down the stages of a task, to support the child to know what to do and so they can track their progress through the task.

- <u>Now and next cards:</u> These use visual prompts to demonstrate to a child what they are doing now and what they will need to do next. This reduces anxiety and uncertainty, so supports transitions. These can work on a broad subject level, such as 'Now: maths, next: English', though some children need these to be more specific so they can identify phases or activities within a lesson. Some children respond better to 'If… then…' prompts, e.g. if they complete an adult-directed task, then they can do one of their choice.

- <u>Visual timetables:</u> These are commonly used in primary classrooms so the class know what is happening. Many children with SEND benefit from an individual visual timetable, as they struggle to see themselves as part of the class and/or their timetable is different to the majority of the class.

- <u>Worked examples:</u> This is a modelled example that the child can copy and then alter slightly, for example a maths calculation where the child repeats the method with different numbers, or a sentence in which the child changes key words.

There is more about these approaches in Chapter 5.

If we make the support visual, we reduce the need for your TAs to be constantly at the child's side or repeat information and instructions. Your TA repeating instructions verbally can lead to confusion. They may express your instructions differently or use different vocabulary. This can make the task more difficult for the child to understand, particularly if they have language or communication difficulties, as they try to process and compare different versions of the same information. This can further increase dependence on a TA and inhibit learning.

If this isn't working…	…try this
Hadi sat with his TA, Ruth, at the side of the room. During the teacher input, Ruth would constantly have to prompt Hadi to listen, repeating what the teacher said. This disrupted the learning for Hadi and the rest of the class. During individual working, Ruth would need to prompt Hadi to remind him of every step of the process. Hadi was dependent on Ruth's prompting for all his learning.	The class teacher moved Hadi to sit near the front and put a small visual reminder, showing him sitting and paying attention, on the edge of the board. The teacher tapped this when she needed to remind Hadi to focus. She and Ruth agreed a key question for each lesson. Ruth then worked with Hadi to prepare an answer. Hadi loved listening for and answering 'his question'. After the input, Ruth would take Hadi for a quick movement break, before setting up his task management board with him, going through the instructions again and making a checklist of what Hadi needed to do. As he completed each part of the task, he ticked it off.

The helicopter approach may mean your TA preparing resources, providing pre- and over-learning (see Chapter 6 for more details) and supporting the development of IT skills and other interventions to promote independence. This may mean that they are less visible in the classroom. They are not offering less support but offering it in a different way, enabling children to become more independent. If you deploy your TA in this way, it needs to be clear to both them and others what they are doing and how the resources promote learning.

Case study

Although he had lots of ideas, Yotam struggled with writing. He was becoming increasingly dependent on his TA, Claudia, to scribe for him. It was decided that Yotam should use IT more so he could record more independently. To support this, he had a daily session using a typing programme to develop his familiarity with the keyboard and ability to type. It was also decided that he should use a sentence-building programme that would offer him a choice of key vocabulary to support his writing. However, the subject-specific vocabulary needed to be entered into the software, ready for him to use. This meant that Claudia spent 15 to 20 minutes each week out of the classroom, setting up the word banks on the computer programme ready for Yotam. Claudia was not working directly with him but was creating the resources to enable him to be more independent.

Building a team around the child

A key element of moving away from the 'Velcro® TA' model is building a team around the child. Fundamental to this is ensuring that all

SEND children have time with you, their teacher, and that any adult in the room can and does work with any child. This can be your TA 'releasing' you to work with SEND children, by them undertaking the roving support role in the classroom.

Moving away from the 'Velcro® TA' model means it is essential that you find time with your TA on a regular basis to discuss your SEND children. You need to have a shared sense of how the children are progressing, in order to determine whether the support you are providing is working and plan any additional or different support that may be required.

However, if your TA's training has been focused on specific forms of SEND or interventions to be used with a particular child, we are at risk of falling into the 'training trap'. This is where a member of staff is trained to deliver a specific intervention and takes full responsibility for it, meaning that you do not know what your TA is doing or why. This can easily extend, so that as the TA takes on responsibility for meeting some of the child's needs, they become, by default, liable for *all* their needs, regardless of their training or capacity to do so. This can lead to separation between you and the child, and the TA.

Not only can a child develop dependence on a TA when they work together to the exclusion of others, but the TA can become dependent on the child for their place and sense of value in the school community. On occasions, this relationship can tip over into safeguarding concerns.

Case study

Matt was a wheelchair user and needed support with his physical needs and intimate care. He was supported by a team of adults in and out of the class. This was led by Cherry, who had worked with Matt since Year R. In Year 4, it became clear, as Matt's health deteriorated, that he was going to need more specialist physical and medical support. It was agreed with his parents and the LA that he would move to a specialist setting for Year 5. Cherry quickly became distraught. She applied for a job at the specialist setting, saying that she wanted to continue to work with Matt. The specialist setting was concerned that Cherry was unable to separate from Matt and asked whether there were safeguarding concerns about their relationship.

When the head addressed this with Cherry, it quickly became clear that she lacked confidence to undertake other roles in the school and felt that if she was not working with Matt, she would not have a role in the school.

Over Matt's final term in the mainstream setting, it was arranged that Cherry would work less with him, and she was supported to work with a range of other children and develop her skills. This also enabled Matt to develop his independence away from Cherry, ready for his move to his new school.

Changing the language from one-to-one to 'key person'

Building a team around the child is supported by a move away from the language of a one-to-one support to describe a single TA working solely with a particular child. The child can still have a 'key person' who is the main contact point and 'holds the child in mind', as we do in Early Years classes. But they are part of a team who share the education, information and care of the child. Using the language of a 'key person' can provide the support and security that many children and parents need around the provision for a child with SEND, without the need for a nominated one-to-one TA or the implications and expectations that the child and adult will work only together to the exclusion of others.

If this isn't working…	…try this
Noah was a bright and engaged pupil who had a medical condition that required daily medication and twice-daily physio activities. Olivia was trained to deliver these supports. This meant that she was based in Noah's class.	It was clear that Noah had specialist medical needs and needed additional non-pedagogical support. In the general run of things, he did not need learning support, though it was important that support was available to help him catch up after absences.
After Noah had an operation and missed some weeks of school, Olivia worked with Noah to make up the work he had missed. Increasingly, she worked with Noah and became the 'expert' on his condition. She also developed a close relationship with Noah's mum, who used her as a sounding board to discuss possible further treatments and their impact.	It was agreed that Olivia would be Noah's key person and the main contact for his mum. But it was also agreed that both Olivia and Maggie, the class TA, would attend all the training for Noah's medical and physio needs. The class teacher and SENCo also received a briefing, so everyone knew what was happening.
During Noah's time in Year 5, Olivia was admitted to hospital for emergency treatment and was off work for about six weeks. Only at this point did it become clear how little anyone else in the school knew about Noah and his needs.	It was agreed that Maggie should provide Noah's support two days a week, so that she could practise what she had been trained to do and to give Noah and Olivia a break from each other.

Sharing information to build a picture of the whole child

Too often when we are working with children with SEND, we become focused on what they can't do and what they find difficult, so we miss their strengths and motivators. In order to fulfil their role, every adult in the school team around the child (the SENCo, teacher and TAs) needs to have a clear and shared understanding of the whole child. By identifying the child's strengths and interests, we can use these to mitigate the barriers to their learning.

It is useful to work with your TA (and, if possible, the SENCo and/or parents) to create a pupil profile to share and collate information about the child. This template pupil profile could be used as a starting point.

| **Their strengths:** What are they good at? **Their motivators:** What are they interested in? What do they enjoy? | Replace with a photo of the child Name: | **Their barriers to learning:** What is getting in the way of their learning? What is it they find difficult? Think specifics. **Their needs, difficulties and weaknesses:** What specific things do they struggle with? What particular areas of learning do they struggle with and need support with? What support do they need to help them access learning and develop independence? |

Understanding different roles

To build an effective team around a SEND child, it is essential not only that we share information but also that the different staff involved understand their roles and how they best work together to meet the child's needs. The table below provides a useful framework to help with this, though the exact roles will vary from school to school.

SENCo	Teacher	TA
To support whole-school planning and provision for children with SEND, providing strategies and resources to support individuals and groups.	To plan learning for the whole class, including differentiation for individuals and groups.	Working from the teacher's plans to put into place specific strategies to support individuals and groups' learning and wellbeing.
To work with other people in school, including teachers, TAs and other professionals, to set targets for the child.	To use the child's targets to plan for their learning and understand their needs.	To use the child's targets to focus on particular skills the child is working on.
To identify appropriate interventions, strategies and resources for a child.	To plan for any interventions a child may take part in (in or out of the classroom) while ensuring all children access quality teacher time and input, including the use of appropriate strategies.	To follow plans for and keep records of any interventions they run (in or out of the classroom), following the agreed strategies under the teacher's direction.

SENCo	Teacher	TA
To ensure all statutory paperwork is completed for the child.	To feed into the statutory paperwork, particularly termly and annual reviews. To plan any additional support the child will need to access assessments.	To share with the teacher how the child learned in the lesson, what they found difficult and what their areas of success were.
To observe the child and then provide ideas about how best to support them.	To manage behaviour in the classroom.	To support their focus child to manage their anxiety levels and emotions successfully.
To liaise with other professionals working with the child, e.g. SALT, OT, EP.	To feed into liaison with other professionals, sharing feedback and ensuring the appropriate support is in place.	To follow and implement the strategies agreed by the teacher, SENCo and other professionals, including providing feedback.

Developing a common language for monitoring and identifying progress

All these roles need to be involved in and feed into the 'Assess, Plan, Do, Review' cycle that is key for planning for, identifying and promoting the learning, attainment and progress of children with SEND.

Assess → Plan → Do → Review

- **Assess:** Where is the child working? This does not need to be a formal assessment.
- **Plan:** What are we going to do about this?
- **Do:** The actions in response to the assessment and planning.
- **Review:** What has been the impact? What has worked well? How can things be changed to work even better?

Many children with SEND consistently work below age and national expectations in some, if not all, areas. This makes their progress more difficult to identify and record; however, it does not mean that they are not making progress. For many children, this progress may be small steps and often hard to see.

To identify their progress, we need to develop a shared language to describe learning with our TAs. We need to focus on what children can now do, know or understand that they couldn't in the past. It is a matter of working from where the child is and was: comparing them to themselves, rather than the national criteria. Also, we should try to consider all areas of the child's life, including their academic achievements, rather than solely focusing on these. Their progress might be evidenced by their:

- learning
- engagement in the classroom and beyond

- social interactions
- willingness and/or ability to do things independently
- self-help and organisational skills,
- physical skills
- behaviour and resilience
- enthusiasm.

This learning and progress is often recorded through specialist SEND targets. Different schools set, record and monitor SEND targets in different ways. Most schools share and record SEND targets through some form of individual support plan. At one time, these were all known as IEPs (individual education plans), but this language was changed with the 2015 Code of Practice, and they might be called ISPs (individual support plans), pupil passports or profiles or something else. Regardless of the name, their role is to record:

- the child's targets or outcomes (these should be SMART targets: Specific, Measurable, Achievable, Realistic and Timely)
- the provisions and actions to help them achieve these targets or outcomes
- an evaluation to support planning next steps;
- a review date.

Schools may include other information, such as costings; which staff are responsible for particular parts of the plan; multi-agency involvement; and child and parent comments.

If a TA is going to support a child with SEND effectively, they need to understand and contribute to these plans and targets. Regardless of the format used for the plan, it needs to be a working document that all staff can and are expected to contribute to. Different schools have their own ways for staff to contribute to discussions about children's progress, but it is key that you try to find ways that work for you and your TA. This might be by the TA:

- adding notes either directly or using sticky notes on a shared version of the plan
- annotating their own version of the plan
- contributing to review meetings
- sharing information verbally.

Helping children to identify their progress

Children's progress is often small-step, gradual and incremental, so it is hard to identify. This is why regular reviews are important. The process of stopping periodically and actively looking at children's progress and achievement can be supported by:

- looking back in children's books and comparing work over time
- using photos or 'Marvellous Moments' books to record successes (both academic and non-academic) to build achievement
- making proactive use of the children's SMART targets
- being aware of learning objectives or intentions and using these to highlight what a child has done, rather than focusing on what they have not.

It is key that we and our TAs can and do recognise children's progress so that we can support children to identify their own successes and develop a sense of accomplishment and pride in their work. For example, we can:

- Use specific praise to highlight the change in their learning, e.g. 'I like the way you did…' or 'Do you remember that last week you struggled to do… but now you can…'.
- Use photos or evidence from their books to demonstrate their progress.
- Express any measurement against their targets in child-friendly language.

- Support the child to share successes with others: staff, other children and their parents.
- Sometimes it can be hard for children to accept praise and recognition of their progress, so sharing it with someone else within the child's hearing can work well.

If this isn't working…	…try this
Nora worked as a TA and believed that she had a clear understanding of learning. If a child learned their spellings, they would score well in a spelling test and then they would be able to spell the words. She was hugely frustrated when she was working with Sally, who consistently got nine out of ten in her spelling tests but would fail to spell the same words accurately in her writing. Nora felt that Sally must be doing this deliberately and not trying. She regularly became angry with her.	The SENCo met with Nora and discussed how, while Sally could learn and recall words in a test situation where that was the focus of the activity, she struggled to apply this when faced with the multiplicity of skills required for writing (e.g. handwriting, sentence construction, word choices, remembering her ideas). They then worked with the class teacher to set a target for Sally about spelling, which identified a list of key words that Sally would work to spell correctly, consistently and independently in her writing. This was supported by 'focused editing', where Sally was supported to check three key words in her writing by having them on a card beside her. When she was editing her work, she would identify and circle each time she had used a key word, then either tick it or correct it. Over time, Sally began to embed her spellings into her writing and Nora became less frustrated, as she could see that Sally was making progress.

Conclusion

The understanding and sharing of a child's learning are key to successful support for children with SEND, so that all the adults in the room can work effectively with them. In this way, they do not become isolated or excluded from either the teacher or their peers. We need to try to move away from the 'Maslow's hammer' (Giangreco, 2021) approach to SEND support, where the only tool we have is a hammer so we treat everything as if it were a nail: children with SEND need a range of supports and strategies, not just TA support. Too often this feels like the easiest path, so we fall back on it. We need to remember that support and provision for children with SEND (at SEN Support or EHCP level) need to be personalised to meet the child's needs. The support needs to fit the child rather than expecting the child to fit the provision. The provision needs to be constantly reviewed, evaluated and adjusted accordingly. For this to be effective, we need a team working around the child, including the teacher and TA working together, rather than a position where the education of children with SEND becomes outsourced to TAs.

Key points to remember:

- Support for children should be personalised, based on their needs and adjusted in response as their needs change.
- All children are entitled to teacher time; work with your TA to ensure you retain an overview and retain key responsibility for all the children in your class.
- TAs have a key role to play in supporting learning in the classroom. They may:
  - be working with a child one-to-one
  - work with groups of children, e.g. children with SEND, higher achieving children or children receiving pupil premium

- swap in with you to enable you to work with any of these children.
- To work together, it is key that teachers and TAs have a shared understanding and knowledge of the children in their care.

Things to discuss with senior leaders

It will vary from school to school who takes the lead on TA deployment. It is important to work out who this is, so that you can discuss how to best work with the TAs in your class. It might be the head or deputy head, the SENCo or even the business manager.

- Consider the best model of TA deployment in your classroom to support the children in your care and discuss this with senior leaders.
- There will be a number of other professionals who may be involved in the child's support, particularly if they have an EHCP. How should these professionals work with you and your TA, so information is shared effectively?

Things to think about

- How well do you know your children with SEND?
- How much time do you spend with these children compared to other children in the class?
- Do you understand the interventions and support being provided for the children in your class by your TA and other agencies? Remember that, as the teacher, you remain responsible for their learning.

Things that work really well

- Often conversations with TAs become focused on what children with SEND can't do and it is easy to miss their strengths and motivators. Using a pupil profile is a good way of capturing and sharing key information about children.
- It is often possible to incorporate therapy activities and interventions for specific children into the learning for the whole class. For example, when a speech and language therapist (SALT) asks children to work on specific sounds or identifying syllables, this can be included in whole-class or small-group phonics sessions, or particular stretches recommended as part of a physio programme can be included in PE lessons. This both provides support and promotes inclusion.

3 Supporting home–school communication

'My TA became the parents' "go-to" person. She had time to listen and then shared what she had learned with me and others – the SENCo, the DSL, etc. – when needed. By supporting the parents, she was able to make a real difference to the children.'

Teacher

For children to feel safe, they need to feel that the adults in their lives are working together. Those of us at school cannot match children's parents, carers or guardians' impact on their lives, so it is vital that we engage with them (Early Years Coalition, 2021). Through effective home–school communications, we can make children feel safe and supported, so they are more able to learn effectively.

In Early Years, we talk about creating a triangle of trust around the child, where all those involved with the child's learning work

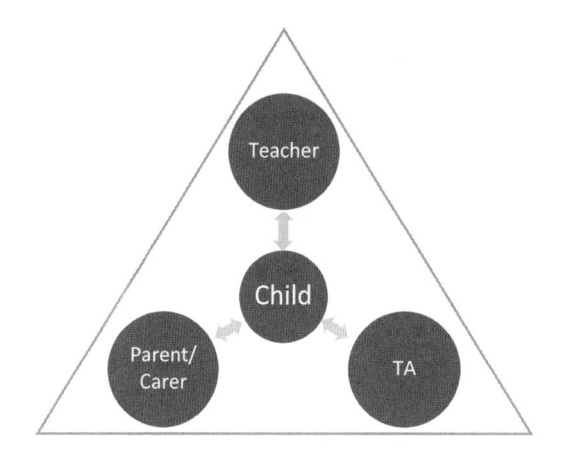

The triangle of trust

together to support them. We need to continue this into primary school, giving a voice to all those involved in a child's learning and recognising the importance of communication between them.

If this triangle of trust is to be effective, we and our TAs need to understand that:

- Children do not turn up in our classrooms as a blank sheet. They are impacted by what goes on outside the classroom, particularly at home. We need to consider this when we are thinking about children's learning and behaviour and how best to support them.
- Communication needs to be a two-way process. We need to listen to parents as well as informing them about what is happening with their children at school. They are the experts on their child. It is very easy to disregard or disbelieve parents when they describe their child differently to the way that you see them. They are seeing them differently because children are different in different settings and with different people.

Case study

Chaya was very quiet and studious in school, almost withdrawn. Her teacher, Evie, was astonished at parents' evening when Chaya's parents described her temper tantrums, meltdowns and aggression at home. Evie shared this the next day with Carol, her TA. Carol felt that there must be something wrong with their parenting and suggested that Evie should speak to the HSLW (home school link worker) about a parenting course. Evie added this to her 'to-do list'.

A few days later, a rather shamefaced Carol told Evie that she had seen a TV programme about a celebrity with autism. They had described themselves as being just like Chaya when they were a child. Carol had Googled 'autism in girls' and 'masking behaviours' following the programme. She now wondered whether this was the issue with Chaya.

Evie and Carol spoke to the SENCo, who explained that the school could not diagnose autism, but she would talk to the parents.

After meeting with the parents, the SENCo was able to support them with a referral to CAMHS (child and adolescent mental health services) and some strategies to use with Chaya at home. She also gave Evie and Carol strategies to use to help manage Chaya's anxieties in school (which were causing her to be withdrawn), so that she was calmer at home.

Recognising the importance of home–school communication

Your school will have guidance and protocols that govern how you and your TAs communicate with parents. These will vary from school to school. Some schools operate an 'open door' policy, where teachers and other staff are freely available to talk to parents at the school gate or classroom door; others work on a strictly appointment-only basis. Some provide all parents with the teachers' emails; for others, all communications must go through the school office. There are umpteen variations in between.

Most schools have elements of the following.

- formal communication through:
  - annual (or more frequent) written reports
  - meetings called to discuss specific issues
  - regular set meetings, including parents' evenings and SEND reviews

- written information (either in hard copy or online) to the whole school or classes
- written information for individuals, including reading records and SEND plans
- informal communication through:
  - meetings at the gate, classroom door or on the playground
  - phone calls
  - written information through notes in book bags and/or planners, emails and home–school communication books.

Often our face-to-face communication is time-bound and quick, either at parents' evenings or at the school gate. This means that there is a high risk of misunderstanding and misinterpretation on both sides, which can impact our relationships, particularly when dealing with sensitive issues or when there are multiple people involved. We need to remember that, for parents, almost all messages about their child are sensitive, even when we think that they are mundane.

If this isn't working...	...try this
Arlo was on the SEND register. Both his parents and teacher had concerns about his speech. The SENCo wanted to refer him to SALT (speech and language therapy) and needed parental permission. She gave the permission form to the class teacher and asked her to catch Arlo's parents, explain what was happening and ask them to sign the form.	The SENCo met Arlo's parents and explained what the SALT would do and how the system worked, including that it would be some time before the SALT came into school and that she would let them know when this was happening. The class teacher and the TA then both repeated the same message.

The teacher gave the form to the TA who was on the door and asked her to get Arlo's parents to sign the form, which his mum did.	Nevertheless, Arlo's dad contacted the school regularly to check when the SALT would come, but he did so more calmly, as the message had been consistent and not gone through Arlo.
A week later, Arlo's dad called the SENCo, upset that the doctor had seen Arlo without either parent being told. It took a long time to understand that Arlo had told his father that someone had come to see him in school and his dad had assumed it was the SALT, who he thought was a doctor. In fact, the visitor was the vicar, who had talked to the whole class.	

Using TAs to support communication

In most cases, TA involvement is part of the informal communications, though it is often helpful to have them at more formal meetings if possible, particularly where they provide a specific intervention or support.

In many schools, there are a range of support staff including HSLWs, EAL and office staff, who, even when they are not formally employed in this role or in the classroom, can support and facilitate home–school communications. Additionally, they may be recruited from the local community and have clear links to and understanding of it.

We need to be aware that it can be difficult for members of staff who feel that they have a foot in both the school and local community camps. There may be times when they feel torn between their role in school and their relationships outside school. This can lead to issues of confidentiality when parents talk to TAs about school issues away from the school site.

'It was difficult going from "just" a parent to a volunteer to a paid member of staff. I never felt I was fully part of the school community because I was always wearing my parent hat.'

TA

However friendly and smiley we are, there are many parents who, for different reasons (sometimes to do with their own experiences at school), find talking to school staff, particularly teachers, intimidating and scary. Some of these will respond by not engaging with us and others by being defensive or aggressive. Other parents will be very conscious of how busy you are and don't want to infringe on your time. This means that some parents find it easier to speak to your TAs – and sometimes TAs may have more time to stop and chat.

Additionally, sometimes TAs can be easier to find without having to enter the school building, as they are often involved in breakfast and after-school clubs. Also, speaking to a TA can often be done without dealing with emails and websites, which can be an issue for less literate or tech-savvy parents.

Case study

Cassie came from the Traveller community and had not really attended school herself. However, she was keen that her children should both attend school and do well there. She wanted to be involved in their learning but was very nervous about her communications with the school. She was worried that they would judge her spelling and handwriting. Although she could text, she was not confident using email. Cassie much preferred to talk to someone, ideally not a teacher.

After a long and tearful conversation with the head after one of her children had been in trouble, the school developed a better understanding of how best to communicate with and involve Cassie. They set up a system where she had a 'key person' TA, who was able to make time to talk to her and then share her communications back to the teaching staff. As their relationship developed, the TA supported Cassie to attend parents' evenings and eventually adult education classes.

Using the 'key person' approach

The idea of a key person is an integral part of the Early Years. They help the child to feel emotionally secure when away from home and provide a reassuring and consistent point of contact for parents. This remains important for children and their parents throughout their school career. A TA or teacher can undertake this role.

Often when schools are communicating with parents, there is an issue as too many people are involved: the teacher, the TA, the SENCo, the headteacher, a member of the pastoral team, someone from the office and so on. This means that messages sometimes get lost or are never delivered, as everyone assumes someone else has spoken to the parents. Also, it means the parents are often not sure whom to communicate with or who is responsible for what, and they are never certain that the key information has reached the right person. Moreover, they are constantly having to repeat their family story.

If this isn't working…	…try this
Georgina's son Drew had special needs and regularly struggled to come into school. He often had to be 'peeled off' her by a member of staff. Both Georgina and Lewis found this very distressing. Georgina's distress was increased by the fact that this was done by	It was recognised that Drew struggled with coming into school. After a meeting with the teacher, class TA and SENCo, it was agreed that Drew would come in through the school office rather than waiting on the playground. He would be met each day by his key person, a TA, who

| different staff on different days, and each time she had to explain the issue over Drew's howls. | would take him to the classroom, where he could read quietly until the other children came in. Georgina was able to email the teacher directly on days when Lewis was particularly anxious and explain the reasons. As soon as this system was set up, both Georgina and Drew's anxiety decreased, and increasingly Drew was able to come into school calmly. Over time, Drew gained his confidence to come in with the other children, but it was a slow process. |

Supporting children with SEND

For children with SEND, the key person approach provides a clear first point of contact. Although parents often expect a TA to be employed full-time to work with their SEND child, in reality support is usually provided across groups of pupils or only in particular lessons. Clear communication from a key person (a teacher or a TA) can support parents both to have a realistic idea of what happens in school and not have unrealistic expectations of their child's abilities. This approach can often help mitigate parents' concerns about their child not having a 'Velcro®' TA.

Case study

Liam had an EHCP with provision for full-time support. In fact, Liam could work independently after a prompted start in many lessons and was increasingly able to manage on the playground, providing he was able to go to his key person if he began to feel overwhelmed or anxious. Liam's parents were happy that Liam had 'helicopter' support and that 'his' TA worked with other children as well as Liam.

However, towards the end of each term, his mum would send a flurry of emails to the SENCo and his teacher and catch his TA to discuss his support for the following term. Also, Liam's anxiety levels would begin to increase.

When the teacher and SENCo spoke to Liam's mum, she would immediately be reassured that the support would remain unchanged. In fact, she freely admitted that she became anxious about transitions, which is why she needed to check everything was in place for the next term. As soon as the school supported her, Liam's level of anxiety also decreased.

For children with SEND, the triangle of trust needs to be extended to include the SENCo. It may need to include other multi-agency colleagues, such as speech and language therapists, occupational therapists (OTs) and educational psychologists (EPs).

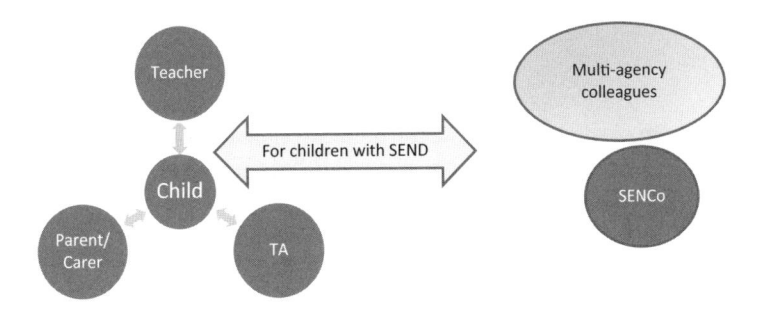

While the SENCo will have oversight of their involvement and it is vital that you understand the provision and support for the children with SEND in your class, it is not always easy for teachers to meet with all the agencies and professionals involved. This often means that the TA becomes the pivotal point of contact and liaison for parents and the multi-agency colleagues working with a child, managing the day-to-day communications and implementing the recommended strategies. Often, they become the key person responsible for sharing the strategies with parents. If so, they need to be supported to do this. This can include the following:

- Identified time for the communication. It is not appropriate to discuss the details of therapy or personal care at the school gate as other children and parents come past. This could be a face-to-face meeting or via a phone call or online meeting.

- Ensuring that the TA understands what they are communicating. Too often, they are given a short session with a professional and then expected to both implement and explain the strategies to others. They should be supported in this by the SENCo or another professional.

- A chance to practise an explanation by sharing it with you (or another member of staff) before they speak to the parents. It is better that you ask questions, and they can find or work out the answers if needed, than being asked by the parent and not knowing.

- Supporting the verbal communication with something written and/or visual that the parent can take away to remind them of what has been said – but don't depend on written communication on its own being clear to the parent.

If this isn't working…	…try this
Zarann had significant fine motor skill difficulties, which impacted his access to daily tasks. The OT came into school and worked with him and Amelia, the class TA, setting up various exercises to develop his skills and the strength in his hands. Zarann needed to do these daily at home and at school. The OT left a sheet showing the exercises and asked Amelia to share it with his parents. Amelia met Zarann's mum and showed her the sheet and tried to explain it, but he did not do the exercises at home.	Amelia discussed with the class teacher and SENCo the best way to share the information with Zarann's parents. They were invited into school for a meeting after drop-off. Amelia then went through the sheet, demonstrating each exercise with Zarann. As they did this, his mum made notes on her own sheet. Not only did they have some fun practising the exercises together, but Zarann also continued them at home with his mum.

Where a TA has worked with a named child over a number of years, they often become the expert on that child, developing a close relationship with the child and often with their parents, which can make it difficult to change the way the child is supported or how home–school communications work. There is a risk that the TA can become a 'gatekeeper', holding all the key information about the child and acting as the sole conduit for it. Further, there can be issues of boundaries between the family and TA, effectively separating both the child and their parents from the teacher.

Case study

Edith had supported Emily, who was a wheelchair user with physical and cognitive difficulties, for many years.

> She was Angie, Emily's mum's, key person in school, and increasingly she would discuss both school and medical matters with her.
>
> During Year 5, it became clear that Edith and Angie were meeting for coffee out of school on a regular basis, and the relationship had moved beyond the professional. Angie benefited from a friendship with someone who understood her daughter and her needs. However, their relationship made it increasingly difficult for Edith to support Emily in school effectively and professionally. Emily felt that anything she said or did was immediately reported to her mum. Ultimately, this could have inhibited Edith's ability to ensure that Emily's welfare was paramount and maintain a robust approach to support her safeguarding.

While their key person may be a parent's first point of contact, we need to ensure that they are not their only point of contact. All parents are entitled to direct communication about their child's learning and welfare with their teacher.

Managing expectations through clear and consistent messaging

Without clear information-sharing between staff, there is a danger of confusion. There are risks that an informal conversation with a TA can set up expectations from parents that things should and/or will be actioned, but this is not always appropriate, possible or communicated to the teacher.

> **Case study**
>
> Anthea had worked in the school as a TA for many years and was a popular and respected figure with staff and parents. Richie and Amal, two boys in her Year 4 class, were constantly having arguments and falling out. One day, Amal's mum approached Anthea and shared that Richie had been using racist language to Amal. She was very upset and wanted something done at once.
>
> A few days later, Amal's mum approached the headteacher to find out what had happened about the racist language. She was quick to point out that she didn't want Richie to get into trouble, but she did want him to understand how upsetting it was. The head naturally looked confused and had to ask to whom she had spoken about it. The mother pointed to Anthea.
>
> When the head spoke to Anthea, she said that the mum had spoken to her, then Anthea had spoken to the boys and it was all dealt with. The head had to explain that all racist incidents need to be recorded and that this should have been discussed with the class teacher and headteacher.

In this case, Anthea was unaware of the significance of the incident or the importance of sharing this information with the class teacher and, in this case, the head.

Making communications work

We need to be aware of the dangers of disguised compliance, where a parent shares different information with different staff or even attempts to play staff off against each other by saying that different people have agreed to different things. Without shared communication, there is a danger of home–school relationships feeling like a power game over who holds more information.

If this isn't working…	…try this
Effie was an ECT working in one of two Year 4 classes. Tammy, her TA, had a daughter in the other class. This made Effie rather anxious, particularly as Tammy would report to her what the parents thought about the activities in her daughter's class and the homework that was set. She was constantly wondering what was being said about her but was scared to ask. She realised that this was beginning to impact on what she was doing in class, and she was constantly second-guessing herself.	Eventually, Effie talked to one of her colleagues about this. They asked whether Tammy was being negative about the other class and Effie realised that she was not. What was making Effie anxious was that the lessons were being discussed at all. However, this was not a bad thing and, in reality, she wanted the children to talk about their learning at home. Effie decided to change tack and started deliberately asking Tammy for feedback about the homework from the parents' point of view. Effie immediately found she had a really useful source of information about what the children were enjoying, what they were finding easy or difficult to do and any difficulties with instructions or resources. She was able to move from feeling threatened by this feedback to being able to use it to improve the children's learning.

Where you and your TA are both involved in communication with parents, you need to keep a shared record of when and what you communicate about so that messages remain clear and consistent. This is difficult, particularly as what may feel like a 'quick word' or yes/no question to you or your TA can feel like a major piece of communication to the family. It can be worth setting up a record system, so that the staff team can note which parents they have spoken to each day.

- Each member of staff has their own sheet to note whom they have spoken to and what about. They can take this out to the playground/gate with them and then return it to a shared file.
- Have a register list where staff mark when they have spoken to a child's parent and what about. This also creates an interesting record of which parents are in regular contact and which staff they prefer to speak to.

Written communication

Different schools have different policies about how TAs are involved in written communications, but in most schools, they will write regularly in reading records and home–school communication books where they exist. It is important that this information is clear and professional.

Case study

Dmitri had a high level of special needs and struggled particularly with anxiety, so it was very important that any events, changes or possible worries were shared between home and school, so that he received consistent and clear messages from both. The class teacher asked Anna, the TA, to write daily in Dmitri's home–school communication book.

However, when she looked at some of the entries, she realised that while the content was mostly clear, they were full of spelling and grammar errors. The teacher was concerned about these going home. There were further issues as Dmitri kept losing the book.

> The teacher had a rethink and agreed with Dmitri's mum that they would exchange a daily email. This meant that either Anna or the teacher could write the entry after school using the spell-check. Also, this meant that there was an electronic record of the messages, so any misunderstanding could be cleared up more easily and Dmitri didn't have to carry the book backwards and forwards.

Unfortunately, sending many daily written home–school communications can quickly become an unmanageable burden, setting up parental expectations that you and your TA may struggle to meet. Furthermore, it's easy for many home–school communication books to become a litany of what has gone wrong. It is often easier to spot and record what has gone wrong, such as meltdowns, behaviour incidents and refusals, than to note everyday successes. The successes are often gradual – writing two more words or reading a bit more fluently – and less easy to spot. A better alternative can be a quick visual timetable divided into short segments with smiley faces to indicate how each session went. For example:

Coming in/ register	1st lesson	Break	2nd lesson	3rd lesson
🙂	😐	😐	😐	🙁
Lunch	Playtime	4th lesson	5th lesson	Comments
🙁	😐	🙂	🙂	Much better after lunch. We will try a snack mid-morning tomorrow and see if this helps.

Then any adult (TA, teacher or staff on the playground) with whom the child has spent the most time in that session can add their view. It takes only seconds and the comment box can be used to add anything noteworthy in more detail. However, if there is a major success or major issue, it is often better to share it in another way.

Being flexible

We and our TAs will often have a preference for either written or verbal communication, ideally within school hours. Unfortunately, this does not always work for the parents. We need to be clear about our workload, but some flexibility is good where possible.

If you can use a smartphone to sign up for things and answer surveys and you are confident with email and social media, you can forget that this is not as easy for everyone. Schools are moving more and more to online communication, but this does not work for all parents and can even be a barrier for some. Equally, some parents will have a preference for written communication as it gives them time to process the information and they have a copy to refer to. Others prefer oral communication as they can ask questions and get immediate feedback.

Equally, we need to be aware of the needs of parents for whom English is not their first language. Even where parents' English appears fluent, they may miss nuances or cultural references or need more time to process what is being said. It is always worth considering whether there is someone within the school community who can support their communications. Try to avoid children acting as translators for their parents.

Personal story

I was working with a family with a little boy with significant special needs. His mum's first language was Lithuanian. Though his mum's English was fine for most purposes, she struggled with

> the technical language about the SEND system. She requested a translator for our next meeting. After much discussion with the local authority and various others, we tracked down a translator. It was only as I got off the phone in the school office that the new admin assistant piped up that she spoke Lithuanian. We had forgotten to check within our own school community for a translator.

Further, for some parents, there might be particular members of staff with whom they prefer to communicate. This might include other support staff, such as the office staff or even the site manager. Widening our team to involve these people can be a good way of supporting some families.

Understanding the boundaries

We need to be aware that the Teachers' Standards sets out clear guidance for teachers about their relationships with other staff and children, but there is no similar guidance for TAs and they often come into the role with little training or guidance. Moreover, their role may mean that their relationship with children is different and more of it may be during less structured times, e.g. on the playground or in the dining hall. There is often a complicating factor that many TAs live within the community and have relationships with the children out of school.

If this isn't working…	…try this
Hugo lived next door to Scarlett, his class TA. He sometimes played with her daughter. Both he and Scarlett found it difficult to navigate the difference between their home	The head had a formal meeting with Scarlett, went through the staff code of conduct and explained what was meant by confidentiality and why it was important.

and school relationships. On several occasions, the headteacher had to remind Scarlett about confidentiality and the importance of not sharing information about children with people outside of school. Hugo tended to call Scarlett by her first name in school, regarded her as his 'person' and would be distressed when she gave others her attention. It was discussed whether Scarlett could continue to work in Hugo's class.

The class teacher and Scarlett went through her role and which children she should work with, to reduce the time she spent with Hugo. Then they wrote a Social Story™ for Hugo, which explained that when Scarlett was wearing her school lanyard she was Ms Cabot, and she was a 'teacher' and she would work with all the children. The class teacher shared the story with Hugo several times and he became happier to 'share' Scarlett with others. He and Scarlett began to recognise her lanyard as 'a badge of office' and indicator that they had a different relationship.

There can be difficulties for TAs (and teachers) who are also parents in the school. It should not make a difference but, in reality, it can, particularly if the possible conflicts of interest are ignored rather than faced up to. Being honest about any issues that arise can be hard but does work. Most parents do know that they see their 'little darling' differently to other children.

Equally, you need to support children to understand that their relationships with adults in school are different to their relationships out of school, even when they are with the same people! You need to be consistent and open, so that you and your TA are both clear and can both explain what is and is not appropriate to children in school, such as sitting on people's laps, the names they are called and so on. We also need to be open to listening to any concerns children may have about adults' behaviour as, sadly, we need to always be prepared to 'think the unthinkable' and consider safeguarding concerns and risks of grooming by staff. Any infringements of the staff code of conduct or possible safeguarding concerns must be discussed with your headteacher.

Conclusion

The way schools work with parents varies from school to school, as does the TA's role in this. TAs have a useful role to play due to their different relationships with children and families. Yet there are dangers that information parents communicate to TAs is not always shared or acted upon, partly due to the lack of time for information-sharing and partly because much of this communication is informal and ad hoc.

Further, you have primary responsibility for the children in your class, and so for communication with their parents, as with learning, your TA should supplement rather than replace you. You need to be clear about the TA's role and how you can both share your knowledge; otherwise there is a significant risk that things will be missed or duplicated.

Key points to remember:

- Follow your school's communication protocols and discuss them with your TA(s).
- For many parents, informal communication with a TA may be easier than more formal communication with teachers, particularly about 'minor' worries.
- Whomever a parent communicates with, there needs to be a system to share information with the whole team supporting the child.
- Remember that, to parents, conversations we see as 'everyday' can be significant; try to understand their perspective on what we communicate.

- Use a range of staff to support your communications with parents and don't rely on a single form of communication working for all parents.

Things to discuss with senior leaders

- How can a 'key person' approach be used to support communication with parents in your class?
- Can your TA play a role at parents' evenings? For children who work closely with a TA, it can be useful to have their input during a parents' evening. However, there may be financial implications to this.
- Are there specific areas, like attendance, where a TA's input would be particularly valuable? How could this be promoted?
- You can learn a huge amount about a child through a home visit, which should not be done on your own if possible, so it is good to take a TA. How could this be facilitated?
- Be aware of risks to TAs if they are being asked to deliver or share 'unpopular' news to families in their community, particularly where safeguarding information is involved.

Things to think about

- How can you be approachable and flexible in communication with parents while considering your own workload? How can your TA help with this?
- What is the best way of sharing home–school communications for you and your TA so that messages remain clear and consistent?
- What are the reasons why parents are not engaging with the school? We need to be careful not to make judgements and

certainly not to blame the children for their parents' lack of engagement.
- How are your TA's views of the community or certain members of it influenced by their own friendships or conflicts within it?

Things that work really well

- If you are lucky enough to have a TA from the local community, use their insight and understanding of the area. If you are new to the area, get them to give you a guided tour, so you know the key places and landmarks.
- Have a whiteboard by your classroom door to record any small notes such as changes in pick-ups, notes about lost property and appointments so on, so that it is easily accessible for staff and information can be recorded quickly and securely.
- If a parent seems upset or bothered, it is almost always worth contacting them sooner rather than later. The longer you leave it, the more their anxiety will increase and the more difficult it will be to defuse and sort out the situation.
- Try to ensure that both you and your TA get to share positive things about a child with their parents. Too often it is the same person discussing behaviour incidents and someone else who gets to share the successes. This can quickly sour the relationship with the person who seems to always share the negatives. It is important to balance positives and negatives and allow for all staff to share both.

4 Supporting learning in the classroom

'We need to resist the urge of jumping in to help or do things for our children. They are more capable than we give them credit for. Allow them to try, give them time to problem-solve and take pride in themselves.'

TA

The teacher and TA need to work as a team in the classroom. Whatever their job title, support staff's primary role should be about enabling, supporting and promoting learning and inclusion, so they need to be involved throughout the lesson. This means that their role is and looks very like that of a teacher.

Separating roles: Teaching and non-teaching roles

The increase in the number of TAs from the 1980s onwards was part of a general increase in paraprofessionals across a range of sectors such as law, health and social care. There remain professional qualifications associated with the 'professional', but for many of those using the services there is little real difference between the professional and other staff. We are now so used to this that we take for granted the fact that many tasks that used to be done by teachers, but which were never really part of their core educational role, are now undertaken by support staff.

> **Personal story**
>
> *As a newly qualified teacher in the late 1980s, I quickly learned that one of the most stressful and time-consuming parts of running any school trip was costing it out, designing the trip letters, and collecting in, counting and balancing the money. After the 2003 National Agreement introduced a list of 25 administrative and clerical tasks that teachers should not be routinely expected to complete, these and many other tasks were passed to the school office and admin staff. It changed my attitude to running school trips.*

Still, many teachers are left feeling overwhelmed by the numerous admin tasks included in their role. However, many are and can be carried out by TAs and other support staff. It is a matter of school policy and culture how TAs are deployed around admin tasks, e.g. who should be doing the photocopying. But we need to recognise this as part of their role in supporting teachers to support children. There are many tasks, carried out by both teachers and TAs, that are not directly connected with the children or their learning, yet are necessary to facilitate successful teaching. These include the basics of communicating about what we are going to teach and how, the preparation of resources and the assessment of learning.

If this isn't working…	…try this
Lisa was becoming increasingly fed up with Tia, her TA. Tia never seemed to be in the classroom when Lisa wanted her to work with the children. She was always 'just' doing something. Much of it was useful, but not what Lisa wanted Tia to be doing.	Lisa sat down with Tia and together they made a list of the jobs that Tia was doing when she was not in the classroom. There were some jobs that Tia didn't need to do, but many of them were useful and necessary. The next step was for Lisa and

| | Tia to work out times each day when Tia could complete these various tasks and the times when she needed to be in the classroom. |

A key element in promoting children's independence in learning is providing the right resources, e.g. visual timetables or 'now and next' boards, to support this. Making these and teaching children to use them may take your TA out of the classroom, but they will still be engaged in supporting learning. There are also tasks directly involved with children and their learning that may happen outside the classroom, e.g. supporting movement breaks, providing SEMH support, SALT interventions or even hearing a child read, as well as providing medical or physical care, or possibly elements of behaviour management.

How you deploy your support staff will depend on the set-up of your school and the numbers of hours allocated to different parts of their role. You need to consider the balance of child-focused and admin roles, to ensure that the majority of your TA's time is spent with children in the classroom. If a task takes your TA out of the classroom, without children, for long periods, perhaps it should be carried out by someone else.

Supporting learning, not task completion

Many TAs feel that they must be seen to be active and engaged, often working with 'their' child, or they could be seen as not doing their job properly. As many of them have had little training in what learning looks like, they can assume that learning and task completion are one and the same. This can cause them to take over the learning and over-prompt children to make sure that the work is finished and the child has something in their book. This is one of the key issues that led research to identify TAs as inhibiting, rather than supporting, learning and inclusion.

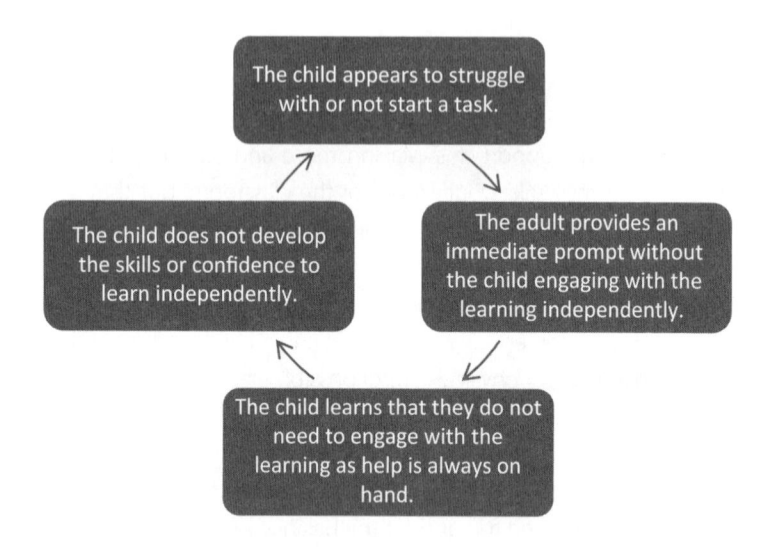

```
                The child appears to struggle
                  with or not start a task.
                    ↗              ↘
The child does not develop         The adult provides an
the skills or confidence to        immediate prompt without
   learn independently.            the child engaging with the
                                   learning independently.
                    ↖              ↙
                The child learns that they do not
                   need to engage with the
                 learning as help is always on
                           hand.
```

Case study

Tabby was a physically disabled student with no voluntary movement below the neck. However, on paper she produced the best artwork in the class because her TA did it for her. This is a focus on task completion, rather than learning, taken to an extreme. There is a danger with this approach that children become like the tourist who has 'done' London, Paris and Berlin in a week. They have been there, seen things, but have no understanding or context. They have just ticked items off on a list. This approach is neither learning nor inclusion.

It is a difficult balance. But we *and* our TAs need to be conscious that the aim is to prompt for independence, not develop prompt-dependence. This includes an acceptance and understanding that a child may access the learning and make progress without completing the task. However, this requires clarity about the process and focus of the learning, which includes your TA being confident that they will not be judged negatively if the child they are working with doesn't complete a task.

If this isn't working...	...try this
Clemmie worked to support a group of children including Zakariya. Zakariya worked very slowly and needed lots of support for processing and recalling information. Clemmie felt under pressure for Zakariya to complete a certain amount of work each lesson, even though Clemmie felt that it was also almost impossible. As a result, Clemmie would end up making suggestions of what Zakariya might want to write by giving her a choice of two ideas, then writing one down and getting her to copy it. As time went on, Clemmie became aware that Zakariya was doing little of the actual learning and was just waiting for her to make suggestions.	Clemmie and the class teacher discussed a new approach. Where possible, they worked from pictures so that Zakariya had a visual prompt for her ideas and could point to things where she was not able to recall the words she wanted. She orally rehearsed her sentence with Clemmie and when she was ready, recorded it on a sound button. This meant she had a reminder of the sentence. She was then encouraged to write it independently. It was a slow process, but gradually Zakariya became more independent and confident to tackle tasks on her own.

As few TAs have more than very limited training to support their understanding of learning, it often falls to us, as the teachers working with them, to fill this gap and develop a shared understanding of learning as a process. It is about the child having sufficient ownership of their learning to enable them to use and apply what they have learned in different contexts, not just finishing a specific task.

Learning from mistakes

A focus on the child's progress and learning needs to include a clear understanding that we learn from making mistakes. We often try to protect children, especially those with SEND, from making mistakes. We worry about the impact on their self-esteem and that it will lead to disengagement or a meltdown. We may even fear that they are 'behind', so don't have time for mistakes. Yet making mistakes challenges and changes our thinking. Furthermore, it supports our teaching as:

- It gives us insight into children's thinking.
- It allows us to identify their misconceptions.

Children cannot learn without the chance to make errors.

Case study

Beth had a diagnosis of autism and she struggled with editing her work. In her view, once it was finished, it was finished. If she was asked to relook at her work, she had a meltdown. It was very tempting not to push this. But that would have severely limited her learning. To overcome this, Beth needed very small steps, starting with very concrete examples, e.g. using a capital I for the pronoun I. By looking at this one thing, Beth was able to develop her tolerance for editing her work. Slowly, she began to accept that the world was still safe when she made a mistake and to be able to learn from her mistakes.

Breaking down the task

Too often when we talk about support for learning, we talk about 'scaffolding'. This has become one of the mysterious terms in teaching that everyone uses and assumes is understood – but it is not always. Scaffolding is about simplifying tasks so that a child can attempt each part by themselves, with specific and structured help where needed. The adult's role is to help the child to know what to do when they are not sure. This may involve reminding them of the strategies they know or could use to solve the problem. It means unlocking their thinking and supporting them to use what they know, but not reminding them at each stage of the process or completing the task for them.

To work, scaffolding needs the following things:

- the task to be broken down into small steps
- effective interaction between the child and adult, including clear and thoughtful questioning, responding to what the child has said or done
- the child to be prompted 'What do you need to do next?', rather than being told
- support for the child to talk through their learning, including what they are doing and why
- the supporting adult to understand the learning and the task fully
- the child to be encouraged to work with the least support they can, so they can take ownership of their learning.

If this isn't working…	…try this
Gemma was in Year 6, but still working at Year 2 levels. The focus was to try to get as many of the class to age expectations as possible. This meant that every time Gemma, who verbalised	It was decided to break Gemma's learning into very small steps, which she was prompted to complete independently using the question: 'What do you need to do next?'

as she worked things out, started to make a noise, the TA shhhed her so she didn't disturb the rest of the class, and pointed her to the answer. This both disturbed the class and stopped Gemma learning, as she became increasingly dependent on the TA's spoon-feeding, which in turn meant that the TA was less able to work with other children.

Sometimes she needed to be given a choice of strategies. Sometimes her independent part of the task was only to write a number or word. But she was able to work independently for a few minutes. The use of the phrase 'Five and I'll be back' reassured Gemma that if she worked independently for a short time, an adult would return.

The staff quickly found that both Gemma's confidence and her independence grew and that her verbalisations were less disturbing to the class than their attempts to stop them.

Sharing the space and positioning to learn

One of the central issues related to supporting learning is how the adults in the room share the space. This is key for modelling effective working relationships but is particularly difficult when the TA enters the room at the same time as the children.

The arrangement of the physical space depends on the culture and practice of your school. Some schools have no teacher desks, while others have desks or at least work spaces for all the adults in the room. Whatever the arrangements, it is important to recognise that if a TA works in your room, they need some space to keep their work materials. Depending on the arrangements in your school, they also may need a safe place to keep their personal belongings, and certainly their coat, especially if they go straight from the classroom onto playground duty.

But more important is how you, the TA(s) and the children interact within the room. While teachers are delivering an input, they tend to stand or sit towards the front of the room, but they also need to consider where the TA is.

- Are they sitting to the side of a focus group/a child?
- If they are working with children who are sitting on the floor, do they sit on the floor with them if they are comfortable to do so, or beside them on a chair?
- From where they are sitting, are they able, without disrupting the learning, to support:
  - engagement in learning?
  - paired talk?
  - with visual prompts to remind children about vocabulary and pre-learning?
  - with behaviour reminders?

Personal story

I was visiting a school to review their SEND support. In every room, I could immediately spot the SEND children because they were always sat to the back and side of the room, with a TA sat between them and their peers. The adults acted as a barrier between these children and their classmates. The SEND children were within the room but excluded from interactions with other children.

Here are some tips on the question of where the TA can sit during structured learning.

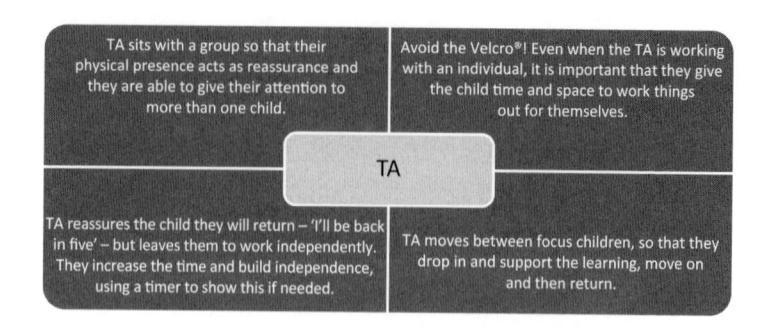

TA sits with a group so that their physical presence acts as reassurance and they are able to give their attention to more than one child.	Avoid the Velcro®! Even when the TA is working with an individual, it is important that they give the child time and space to work things out for themselves.
TA reassures the child they will return – 'I'll be back in five' – but leaves them to work independently. They increase the time and build independence, using a timer to show this if needed.	TA moves between focus children, so that they drop in and support the learning, move on and then return.

(centre: **TA**)

The positioning of TAs in the room and how staff share the space is one of the great unspokens of TA deployment. Whether a TA is sat beside a child or moving and 'working' the room alongside the teacher, it is often assumed that everyone knows how this will work, so it is never discussed. But the silence means that good and shared practice is not developed.

Making questioning effective

Integral to TAs playing an effective role in supporting learning is their use of questioning. A recurring theme in the research on TAs' impact on learning suggests that TAs can be overly reliant on closed questions and dialogue that limits rather than extends children's thinking.

Effective questioning is hard even for those who are trained to understand the process of learning and confident with the subject matter being taught in a particular lesson. So how much harder is it for someone with limited training, who is often picking up the subject knowledge at the same time as the children whom they are supporting? This is why we need to share our planning and identify TAs' level of subject knowledge before we teach. Equally, we need to be clear about the kind of questions we want our TAs to use. This can be done by:

- including prompt questions on our planning
- providing examples of question stems that can be used – Bloom's taxonomy is a good source of ideas

- being clear about the difference between open and closed questions, the different forms of answer they might elicit and when each can be used most effectively.

Linked with this is the importance of 'thinking time' – not expecting children to respond immediately and giving them time to formulate their answers.

If this isn't working…	…try this
Liesl worked to support a small group working significantly below age expectations, including Jimmy, who had slow processing and speech and language difficulties. Halfway through a literacy session, Jimmy burst into tears and ran from the classroom. His teacher settled the others and followed Jimmy out into the cloakroom, where he was kicking things. Eventually, he calmed enough to talk to his teacher and he told her, 'She never lets me answer. She jumps in and takes my words.' Liesl had been trying to help by speeding up the discussion, as it always took Jimmy so long to formulate his ideas.	The teacher explained to Liesl what Jimmy had said and they discussed different ways of giving him thinking time. It was agreed that when she was working with a group, Liesl would: • pre-warn Jimmy of questions, including telling him that she would ask someone else, then him • use visuals to prompt him for key vocabulary • silently count to ten after she asked a question before she expected him to respond.

Using effective strategies to promote inclusion and learning

There are certain basic strategies that TAs can use to support learning throughout the lesson.

Use of visuals

Visuals are a key tool to support the understanding of language and access to learning. While some children can access visuals independently, many need an adult to direct them towards the prompt and/or explain it to them, particularly when it is first introduced.

Prompts for focus and attention

Many children benefit from a visual prompt to remind them to focus on and attend to learning. Often this will be no more than an adult pointing to a picture to remind them about 'good sitting' or 'good listening'. For some children, this may need to be personalised and include a photo of them or something else that is meaningful to them.

Prompts for instructions

A key role for TAs is supporting children's access to instructions. For many children, this requires putting the instructions into a visual form to make them easier to understand and recall. This could be the use of simple pictures or symbols for regular instructions, such as:

| Get your book. | 📕 |

Get your pencil.	
Look at the board, ready to start your work.	

Alternatively, this might be a quick sketch on a whiteboard to remind the child what to do and in what order.

Prompts to support vocabulary development, comprehension and processing

Using visuals can help children with weaknesses in their knowledge, understanding or recall of vocabulary so they engage more easily in learning. This can be done in many ways, including:

- The internet makes it quick and easy to find additional images to support children to access learning. Often it works well when a TA uses a tablet to find and share images to support key vocabulary while you conduct your input.
- When a child has pre-learned key vocabulary, they can have a card to act as a visual reminder or to show to an adult when they have heard or used the word during the lesson.
- The use of vocabulary mats is common in many classrooms, but for these to be effective they need to be relevant, not contain too many words and be supported by clear visuals. They work best when they are reviewed and adjusted regularly to match the child's changing needs and the content of the lesson.

Many children need explicit teaching and modelling before they are able to use visuals effectively to prompt their memory. Visual prompts are most effective when they are memorable for the individual. Unfortunately, many commercially produced prompts are not memorable for children and making personalised prompts takes time, but doing this can be a good use of TA time.

Sensory issues – learning breaks and fiddle objects

Children may need support with sensory regulation at any point in the lesson, including as soon as they have entered the room. Many children, like adults, struggle to sit still. Irritating though their fidgeting and fiddling may be to you, it can often support their engagement and learning. It is important that you and your TA develop a shared approach to children's movement during learning, so that you respond to it consistently. It is good to change the language to talk about fiddle objects that support learning rather than fidget toys, which are things to play with.

'Wobble cushions', 'kick bands', etc. on chairs can support children with sensory regulation, but some children may still need regular movement breaks in addition. In an ideal world, children would learn to manage and organise these for themselves, but the reality is that many children, particularly younger ones, need to be supervised by a TA when they leave the classroom and be supported to engage in any exercises needed.

If this isn't working…	…try this
Felix struggled to sit still and was constantly playing with and/or chewing something. Faye, the class teacher, provided him with a small selection of fiddle objects that she was happy for him to use.	Faye and Mica took some time to discuss Felix and his behaviour during lessons. Faye explained that his fiddling was to meet a sensory need and that he was better able to listen when he was fidgeting.

Mica, the TA, took these things away from Felix as she didn't feel that he was using them 'properly' and was distracting others. Felix then became very confused, upset and frustrated.	Mica admitted that she found Felix's fiddling distracting, so they looked at what Felix could use that worked for him and Mica. After some experimenting and time spent with Felix to explain how to use the different fiddle objects, they settled on a ball of putty, a clothes peg and a piece of furry fabric for him to run his hands over.

Case study

Rhodri needed regular movement breaks to help him to self-regulate and support his focus. When he was in Year 1, he needed a TA both to identify when he needed a break and then to go with him and model the exercises that supported him. By the beginning of Year 2, Rhodri still needed support to know when to take a break but, providing someone stood by the door, he was able to walk up and down and do his exercises independently. In Year 3, most days, Rhodri was able to say when he needed a break and then take it quickly and sensibly, returning to the classroom independently. It was a slow process but, by delivering consistent messages, Rhodri was able to develop independence, which improved his self-esteem and freed the TA to work with others.

Supporting, not creating the curriculum

With a few exceptions – mostly, though not exclusively HLTAs – TAs should be supporting and supplementing teachers, not replacing them or developing their own curriculum or new resources. Your TA's role in supporting differentiation in the classroom should be based on your planning. To do this effectively, your TA needs to understand the learning and lesson content. None of us do our best work when we make it up as we go along or haven't had time to prepare. Pre-learning led by the TA cannot be effective unless the TA is confident with what is going to be taught.

We will look more at ideas for effective sharing of planning in Chapter 7.

Conclusion

The TA's role is to support and point the way, not direct the learning. For a child to learn effectively, they need to have ownership of their learning, feel supported to work independently and be given opportunities and encouragement to try things, including risking making mistakes. Too often, TAs' concern about doing their job and being seen to do it means that children are denied these opportunities. For children to learn, TAs need to have the confidence, ability and understanding of the learning to adapt the task for the children they are working with, not simply ensure that somehow or other it is completed.

There is often an assumption from both sides that we know what a TA does so it is never discussed, but for TAs to support learning effectively, this needs to change. Only by talking and developing a shared understanding of learning and a common language to discuss it can we really support children's learning.

Key points to remember:

- While the teacher should retain ownership of the learning, TAs cannot effectively support learning unless they understand both the learning process and what is being taught in a specific lesson.
- The focus should be on learning, rather than task completion, and independence, rather than prompt-dependence.
- Children need to be able to make mistakes safely to learn.
- Where the TA is positioned in the room needs careful consideration.
- The use of effective questioning from all the adults in the room is key to supporting learning.
- Consistent strategies used regularly can have a huge impact, but they take time to embed and change is unlikely to happen overnight.

Things to discuss with senior leaders

- What is your school's policy about the balance of time TAs spend with children and the time they spend doing admin to support learning?
- There is a view in some schools that if a TA can be 'borrowed', they are not being used effectively. Ignoring the fact that teachers rarely say 'no' to the head and are always willing to try to support a colleague, there are many occasions when 'borrowing' an adult is essential for health and safety. Being able to manage without a TA is evidence that a teacher is 'running the room' effectively. However, if the TA is not missed by the children, then they are not supporting learning.

Things to think about

- Which of the admin tasks you ask your TA to complete directly support learning and which make your life easier? Could anyone else cover any of these tasks to enable your TA to spend longer with the children?
- What does your TA's working space look like and how do they interact with you and the children? Where do they sit? Do they create a physical barrier preventing peer interaction?
- Do you think about how to support the children who learn differently to you and your TA or do you try to impose on them what works for you?

Things that work really well

- Some children are so lacking in confidence or have become so used to adult support that they need a structured approach to develop their independence. For example, use three to five plastic wallets containing simple and familiar activities that the child can do independently, and which are laminated, so any writing can be wiped off and done again. Then give the child set times each day to work through these activities. The activities could include a matching, handwriting or copying activity, a threading/fine motor activity and a simple maths activity. They can build children's confidence that they can do things independently. As they gain confidence, the activities can be changed and more complex ones introduced.
- Ask your TA to monitor your use of questioning – how many open and closed questions do you use within an input or teaching session? This is a great way of focusing them on the difference between open and closed questions and the different impacts that they can have, as well as giving you useful feedback on how to improve your own use of questioning.

5 Support throughout the lesson

'I want to be able to support children from the beginning to the end of the lesson. If I can support them in the first five minutes, so they feel confident, then the rest just works.'

TA

Giving the right support at the right time makes the difference to children and their learning. This means support throughout the lesson, not just at the point when a child has been asked to complete a task. Only providing support at this point misses the importance of the whole lesson for children's learning. To be effective, TAs need to be active and engaged in learning throughout the lesson, not expected to appear and 'support' at certain points. In *The Inclusive Classroom* (2021), Daniel Sobel and I looked at the structure of the lesson in five phases and how to promote inclusion and ensure effective differentiation through small tweaks and adaptions:

1. Transition: entering the classroom and preparing to learn
2. Delivering and receiving instructions and whole-class engagement
3. Individuals working as a class
4. Individuals fitting into a group of learners
5. The last five minutes

In this chapter, I am revisiting this idea, focusing on practical ways in which TAs can support learning during each phase of the lesson.

Phase one of the lesson: Transition, entering the classroom and preparing to learn

| Entering the room | ➡ | Delivering and receiving instructions | ➡ | Individuals working | ➡ | Group learning | ➡ | Last five minutes |

It is often difficult for TAs to be proactive to support learning at the start of the lesson, particularly the start of the day, as many will arrive in the room at the same time as the children. Like the children, they often need a few minutes to get themselves sorted and acclimatised. However, this can be an opportunity for your TA to model the process of getting ready to learn.

Meeting and greeting

At the beginning of the day, it can be useful for your TA to 'cover' the door or gate to take messages from parents and shepherd children into the classroom, while you concentrate on the children. Alternatively, this can be 'flipped' so the TA settles the children while you talk to parents. Either way, there is a real benefit in the TA being involved in meeting and greeting children. The simple process of saying 'hello' and making eye contact, if the child is comfortable to do so, supports the creation of effective relationships within the classroom and allows a quick assessment of where children are and their readiness to learn.

Some children need a personalised 'meet and greet' to help them feel safe to come into the classroom. This can take various forms:

1. Spending a few minutes with an adult as soon as they arrive in the room.
2. Coming in earlier or later than their peers.

3. Coming in through a different entrance.
4. Having a set place in the line and/or walking from the playground to the classroom with an adult.
5. Having a set activity to complete, such as reading, a diary activity, displaying a card to show how they are feeling, a classroom job – any familiar, safe activity to build their confidence for the day.

> **Case study**
>
> Neve struggled with transitions, and coming into school was often difficult. The bustle of the playground and rush as everyone came into school exacerbated this, so it was agreed that Neve would come in through the school office, where she would be met by the class TA. They spent a few minutes in the school library going through the plan for the day and adding this to Neve's individual visual timetable. They would then slip into the classroom part-way through the register, once everyone was quiet and settled. This enabled Neve to come into school calmly and then usually access the rest of the day independently.

Visual timetables

Visual timetables are used in many primary classrooms. They reduce uncertainty and set out the expected routines for the day ahead. Many children benefit from a smaller, personal timetable, using smaller versions of the pictures used for the main class timetable or individual pictures and symbols.

- Some children may not understand that they are part of the group and so how the class timetable applies to them.

- They may struggle to track where they are in the day.
- For those who are going out to intervention groups or therapy sessions, their timetable may be different to the rest of the class; this can add to their confusion if they are expected to both follow the class timetable and recall and understand 'invisible' adjustments.
- Many children benefit from visual tracking through the stages of the lesson.

Some children need the visual timetable broken down into smaller segments, enabling them to focus on 'now' and 'next' or only part of the day.

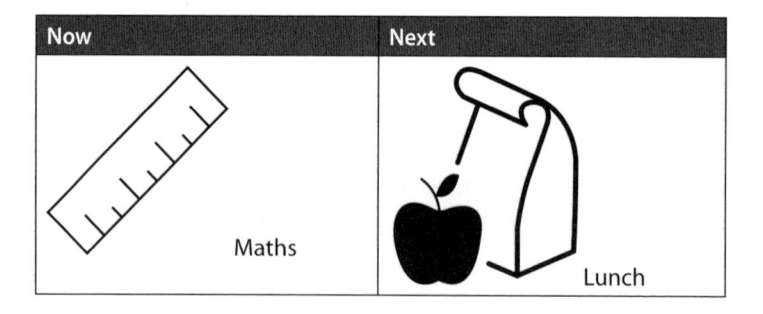

Now	Next
Maths	Lunch

Others need each lesson broken down further so that they know what is expected within the lesson.

For some children, their timetable could simply be a written list that can be ticked or crossed off or rubbed out when the activity is finished. The key element is that the timetable reflects what the child will be doing, particularly if this is not the same as the rest of the class for some of the day, and that it is explained to them by an adult.

Many children struggle with change, particularly the unexpected, for example a fire drill, staff absence or a sudden lesson change due to IT failure or rain. Therefore, whatever form the timetable takes, it is important to introduce and practise the concept of an 'oops' (shown by an 'oops card' that can be added to the timetable) for when things do not go as planned or there are unexpected changes. By practising this with children, we can build their resilience to manage change safely and their understanding that, while upsetting, changes are inevitable and can be managed.

> Oops

Focused interventions

The time while the class are settling is often an ideal point for focused work with individual children. This could include hearing children read, practising tables or handwriting, or supporting them to develop their typing and IT skills. It might include a focus on targets identified on their SEND support plan. The TA can take the register while you lead an intervention group at this point.

If this isn't working…	…try this
Ezra was a newly qualified teacher. He was becoming increasingly stressed by the need to hear children read and could not work out how to fit this into either his or his TA's day.	Ezra set up a whiteboard slide each day setting out a series of 'early morning jobs' for the whole class. This included three children to read to either him or the TA. The other adult then worked with a small group on a pre-learning or over-learning task, while Ezra took the register. Some of the children had particular 'jobs' to do in the morning related to their SEND targets. Some of these children were supported to do this by a peer buddy.

Getting ready for learning

Some children need additional support to get themselves ready for learning. Your TA can usefully work with them to ensure that they are calm and have their equipment ready. This can be supported by a visual.

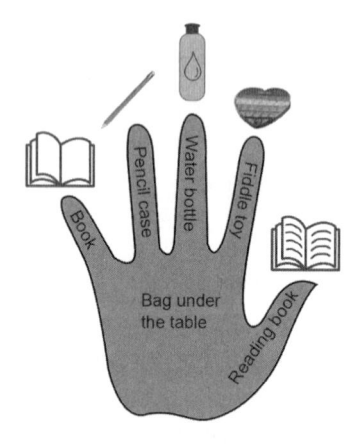

Hand diagram with labels: Book, Pencil case, Water bottle, Fiddle toy, Reading book, Bag under the table

© Rachael Reeves

Phase two: Delivering and receiving instructions and whole-class engagement

Flow diagram: Entering the room → Delivering and receiving instructions → Individuals working → Group learning → Last five minutes

There can be an assumption that when instructions are being given during the teacher input, children are 'only listening' and so don't need TA support. However, this listening is key, and to learn children need to do far more than just listen. For children with difficulties with focus and attention, communication and interaction, etc, this can be the point when learning breaks down, as TAs are often either passive or absent during the teacher input.

Effective support at this phase of the lesson requires both the child and your TA to be present and active in the room. If you don't know what you are doing, it is very hard to do it successfully. But this is regularly the situation we place children in because they were not there for the input or were not supported to access it. However, TAs are often asked to run intervention groups, hear readers or perform admin tasks at this point of the lesson. This means the children who need your TA's prompts for focus and support to understand and access instructions miss out, as the TA is elsewhere. Equally, the children themselves who most need the teacher's input are often absent in these groups.

In addition, TAs need to listen to the input because they are learning new material that they will shortly be expected to teach and differentiate. Ideally, this would not be necessary and the TA could focus on supporting children's learning, rather than using this time to prepare to do so. But, sadly, this is often the reality. If your TA needs to be part of the input to prepare them to support children during individual and group learning, they could:

- record ideas, examples and information or note instructions as a 'flow chart' on a whiteboard or flip chart to support the children's learning later
- effectively co-teach, with the TA modelling the role of the pupil; however, not all TAs or teachers want to do this, nor is it always practical or appropriate.

As we saw in Chapter 4, visuals are key for supporting accessing instruction at this point in the lesson.

Engaging with the input

Oral rehearsal can support engagement with the teaching input. We all worry about getting things wrong, particularly when we have to speak in front of an audience. For some children, speaking in class is a nerve-racking experience. By enabling children to 'rehearse' their ideas or practise a verbal response with an adult before they share it with the class and/or teacher, we reduce their anxieties about what they are going to say or how to say it. It can also help them remember their ideas. Reducing these anxieties means that they are more able to focus on and listen to what you and other children are saying.

Case study

Eliza constantly shouted out, interrupting the class and distracting others. When her teacher talked to her about this, Eliza said that if she did not share her idea at once, she would forget it. It was agreed that Eliza would sit at the edge of the carpet near the TA, and if she had an idea, she would whisper it to the TA, who recorded it on a whiteboard. While this did not stop her shouting out, it reduced it, as she became more confident that there was a record of her idea.

As she became older and a more confident writer, Eliza was able to make notes of her ideas herself.

Alternatively, during pre-learning, your TA can work with a child to prepare an answer for a question you will ask, so that their listening is more focused as they listen for when they will need to offer this information.

> **Case study**
>
> English was not Sami's first language and he struggled to understand what was being said. This was exacerbated by his difficulties with focus and attention. Working with Mina, the TA, his teacher introduced a system of pre-learning. Sami was taught three pieces of key vocabulary with a supporting visual for each lesson. They developed a system where Sami would show Mina the relevant visual when he heard the word. Quickly, both his English vocabulary and his focus and attention improved.

Observations

Your TA has a crucial role to play in working with you to observe and assess the children as they access the input, and identify who is or is not accessing the learning. You may wish to agree the focus of the observations beforehand. It could be:

- assessing a particular focus group or individual
- identifying children who are not understanding the learning, so that they can be given additional input
- looking at behaviour
- focusing on a particular piece of learning or strategy, e.g. which children are counting on their fingers.

Informal observations can be equally valuable. However, both types need to be shared with you to be truly useful.

Phase three: Individuals working as a class

Entering the room → Delivering and receiving instructions → **Individuals working** → Group learning → Last five minutes

The time when children are working on their own or in small groups is often when there are the highest expectations of TA support. At this point, many TAs will take a group out to work on differentiated learning outside the classroom or 'take ownership' of a group in the classroom – often the lower-achieving or those with SEND – and lead and/or differentiate their learning. Each of the latter approaches needs to be considered carefully so they don't inadvertently become a form of segregation, in which the most vulnerable learners are separated from the teacher and responsibility for their learning is outsourced to the TA.

There are many ways that TAs can more effectively support learning within the classroom, which we have already discussed, including:

- a range of different TA deployment models, such as helicopter support and flipping the support
- scaffolding and breaking the task into short segments
- movement breaks
- providing individual visual checklists and now and next cards.

Supporting a focus on the learning, not the admin of the lesson

There is usually a considerable amount of admin involved before a child can start recording their learning, e.g. writing the date and title, drawing a margin or sticking in worksheets. While this is important, it is rarely the focus of the learning. However, for many children this admin can become overwhelming, so they are not able to engage in or, in some cases, even start the actual learning. TAs can support children by completing this for them.

If this isn't working…	…try this
In a science lesson, Ethan and his partner had collected some data about how quickly a toy car went down a slope when it was covered in different materials. They were asked to make a graph to show their different results. Ethan's partner completed this task quickly and used the graph to answer questions about the friction of the different materials. However, Ethan's coordination difficulties meant that he spent the whole time failing to draw the graph and becoming increasingly frustrated.	Instead of Ethan drawing the graph, he could: • work with his partner to create a single graph • be given a blank graph to enter the data on • have an adult draw the graph for him In each of these scenarios, Ethan can record his data and use it to answer the questions about friction, which is the focus of the learning.

A prompted start

Many children struggle to start learning tasks. They need someone to revisit and clarify the instructions and reassure them that they can do it. It is an opportunity for the child to share their understanding of the task and what they need to do. This can be recorded on a task management board.

Task management board		
Task:		
Equipment needed		
	Job	Done
1		
2		

3		
4		
5		

Task management boards can be used with pictures, written lists or a combination of the two.

If needed, the adult can model what the child needs to do, including completing a first calculation or planning sentences together so they don't have a blank sheet when they start writing. Then the child is given time to work independently before the adult returns. Some children benefit from phrases like 'Five minutes and I'll be back' to reassure them that an adult will return and provide more support if needed. Others may need a timer to indicate when the adult will return.

Concrete and visual supports to learn

Many children need access to additional or different support for their learning. For some children with SEND, this may be specific aids and equipment, e.g. particular computer programmes. But they and many other children benefit from concrete resources and apparatus, such as:

- hundred squares, cubes and number lines
- pictures from books and other text as prompts
- photos to help remind them of what they did
- specific word and vocabulary banks, including pictures, so that they can find the words they need easily.

Often, they need an adult to organise, support and model using these resources. It is key that your TAs know what these resources are and how to use them to support children.

Supporting recording

TAs can find themselves acting as an intermediary between you and a child when it comes to demonstrating their understanding. We should be working towards children recording their learning independently, but this is a slow process and we need to ensure that difficulties with recording do not become a barrier to children demonstrating their learning and understanding.

> **Case study**
>
> Hetty loved history and was an excellent historian. She had a superb understanding of chronology, and she could remember key facts and link them to other information to explain historical events. However, Hetty had significant literacy difficulties with spelling, handwriting and punctuation. Her writing was more or less unreadable without mediation.
>
> If we had relied solely on the written evidence, we would have dismissed Hetty's ability as a historian. We needed to find alternative ways for her to demonstrate her understanding and knowledge.

We are at risk in schools of getting into a mindset where we only regard something as learning if it is recorded in the child's handwriting, which leads us to disregard or disparage other ways of recording.

Scribing

All too often, the default for a child like Hetty is for an adult to scribe their ideas for them. Although this does allow them to share their thinking, it is not good preparation for adulthood. It deprives them of the opportunity to develop their own skills for effective communication.

Many children are then asked to copy what has been scribed. I question the purpose of this unless it is a handwriting exercise. If the child has shared their learning, making them copy it out serves little purpose. If we want the child to engage further with the scribed sentence, we can ask them to:

- edit and improve it
- write it onto a strip of paper, cut it up and reorder it, before sticking it into their book
- use it as a cloze exercise for the child to insert key vocabulary.

The use of IT

Few adults write much by hand. At home, many children predominantly use computers. Despite our experiences of remote learning during the Covid lockdowns, we are still ambivalent about the use of computers in the classroom.

There is a further issue that IT use can be seen as a 'magic wand' to solve children's difficulties with recording, but it is not. We consistently underestimate the skills a child needs to develop before they can make effective use of IT, including:

- linking upper and lower case letters
- finding letters on the keyboard
- manipulating their fingers to land on the correct keys
- understanding how to save, file and find their work effectively.

These skills require a high level of cognitive demand and dexterity and, for some, these are unrealistic demands without further support or specialist equipment. For all, it is unrealistic without practice and support.

For children using specialised programmes, the child and the adults working with them need time to develop the skills and understanding to use the software effectively. This can be a challenge. It requires a mindset where we look beyond the one lesson to developing long-term inclusion and independence.

Voice-activated software

Voice-activated software can support recording on computers or other devices, including those that record single sentences or short sections of text. These can often act as an *aide memoire*, supporting a child to remember their idea, so that they can then focus on recording without the need to recall the idea as well.

There are difficulties with these devices where the child's speech is not clear and/or the software picks up background noises. This is always an issue in a busy classroom.

Alternative ways of recording learning

There are many alternatives to writing to record learning, such as:

- using photographs of work
- completing tables and charts
- adding captions and labels to images
- creating PowerPoints and other presentations
- sorting and matching activities
- use of number cards
- mind-mapping.

A quick trip to Early Years is often a good way to be reminded of some of these. We need to remember that for many children, whose struggles with coordination mean they find it hard to write, drawing is no easier, so 'draw a picture' is not an effective alternative.

Supporting self-talk

Self-talk is an essential part of metacognition and enabling children to identify the stages and structure of their learning. Most of us learn to internalise our self-talk, but many children are supported by making this audible. They often need an adult to support this by scaffolding the task, asking what they need to do next and what they already know.

Rewards

Some children find motivation, concentration and recognising they are making progress difficult, so they can benefit from short-term rewards, e.g. a sticker, a thumbs-up, a word of praise, a tick on their work list, etc. It is important that these strategies are used consistently. All the adults in the room need to agree on both how and when rewards are given and stick to it.

In some schools, TAs can be involved in formal marking of the children's books at this point of the lesson.

Phase four: Individuals fitting into a group of learners

Entering the room ▶ Delivering and receiving instructions ▶ Individuals working ▶ **Group learning** ▶ Last five minutes

It can be very easy for adults to take a back seat during group work, but for many children, working with their peers adds a layer of anxiety and difficulty to any task. For those who struggle to understand and/or manage social interactions and communication, asking them to work with others requires them to manage two learning activities simultaneously: academic and social. This can make both more difficult. Additionally, being part of a group makes a child's difficulties more visible to their peers.

Many children need support to understand that they are part of a particular group and need adult prompts both to join their group and to fulfil their role as part of it.

Case study

Whenever his group were asked to leave the carpet, Casey stayed where he was and looked increasingly confused as the children left. He could not remember which group he belonged to. The adults were becoming increasingly frustrated with him and needed a rethink.

When the teacher asked the groups to go to their tables, she displayed a slide showing photos of the children in each group. Casey still struggled, but his peers could remind him, which improved things.

The teacher and TA wanted to move things on further, so Casey was given a personal card listing his groups, which he kept in his tray. After some prompting, Casey began to use this to help him join his group more quickly.

TA modelling and facilitating interactions

Your TA can work with children facilitating interactions and supporting the different roles in a group or during partner work.

If this isn't working...	...try this
Whenever she was asked to work with a partner, Aadya just looked at the floor and refused to respond.	It was agreed that the TA would work with Aadya on some simple written sentence stems that she could use to respond or ask her partner questions without having to speak. This helped her to engage, particularly when she was with a child who she liked to play with on the playground.
	The breakthrough came when the TA drew a quick sketch related to the learning and then Aadya was able to use it to prompt her. She quickly began to add her own drawings and share these with her partner, who was able to comment on them. Aadya would then add details that demonstrated her understanding and response.

It is important that the adult promotes interaction between the children and does not become a replacement for it. There needs to be a clear difference between a TA supporting a child to engage with another child and a TA taking the role as the child's partner and thus possibly becoming a barrier to their inclusion. This can be supported by using:

- learned scripts and sentences
- clear roles within a group, e.g. spokesperson, scribe, resource manager, etc.
- supports for turn-taking in conversations.

The most difficult art is to know when to be silent or to withdraw and allow children to manage their own communications.

TA as observer

A key role for your TA during group work is as an observer. This role is most useful when the TA is clear whom and what they are observing, e.g. oracy, a particular child, the use of tools, turn-taking, etc., and how this information is going to be used either to plan or to support future learning.

Phase five: The last five minutes

At the end of the lesson, your TA's focus is often on tidying up, preparing resources for the next lesson or moving on to the next place they are needed, so their interactions with children are often fleeting and/or focused on organisational issues. But this loses vital learning time, and the lack of support at this point in the lesson can undermine a child's readiness for the next lesson. In many ways, you want your TA to use the same strategies as during the input:

- modelling
- supporting focus
- supporting rehearsal of ideas
- prompting learning.

Supporting children to finish learning

To finish learning and transition calmly to the next task, many children benefit from time warnings about what is going to happen. While many can access the time warnings you give to the whole class, some need an individual time check and clarification of the expectations about the work to be completed in that time. By doing this, your TA can provide additional support for a calm transition for those who need it. However, you need a shared agreement about what counts as finished and the expectations you have of different children's learning so you and your TA don't push for different expectations, confusing the children and undermining each other.

Emotional support and sharing success

Many children struggle to identify what they have done well or when. They often benefit from an individual check-in with an adult to establish this. For some children with low self-esteem their successes need to be noted, so that they can be shared with home or others in school or photographed to put in an 'awesomeness book', which the child can revisit when they are struggling with self-belief. The TA could record this during the last five minutes of the lesson, to support a child to review their learning and identify what they have done well.

Observations and evaluation

Much of the end of the lesson is involved with assessment (formal or informal) of what children have learned during the lesson. Different schools have different policies on TAs' role in marking. Regardless, your TA will have a critical role as an 'extra pair of eyes', making observations about the children's learning and sharing these with you. The difficulty is that often communication about the children's learning is a quick word grabbed as you and/or your TA leave the room.

Leaving the room

Many of our children struggle with transitions, and the end of each lesson is a transition. Some of them will need focused support with this:

- Emotionally – to reduce uncertainty over what will happen next or provide reassurance that the adult will be there the next day and looking forward to seeing them.
- Practically – to manage and organise their belongings. A quick visual or written checklist can make a huge difference with this.

Case study

Arthur had been adopted from care, had a number of SEMH needs and struggled with self-organisation. School ended at 3.00 pm. From about 2.30 pm onwards, Arthur became louder and more visibly anxious. The day often ended with him throwing his belongings about or hitting people.

It was agreed that just after 2.30 pm, Arthur would talk to the class TA and identify what he had done well that day, then he would go and show this to a member of SLT.

When he came back, Arthur helped the teacher and class put up the visual timetable for the next day. He then used a visual checklist to help him gather his belongings into a large bag, so that he could keep his bag, PE kit, lunch box and water bottle all together.

This made Arthur much calmer at the end of the day. After a week or so, he commented that he was worried about who was in the room the next day. It was only at this point that staff realised the impact of there being different staff in the room on different days. They added another step to the routine. Arthur checked the list of who should be working the next day and then added their photos to a visual timetable.

Conclusion

Your TA has a key role in supporting learning throughout the lesson and adapting it to meet the needs of individuals and/or groups of children. You should remain in charge of the whole class throughout the lesson, but you and your TA should be able to swap roles to ensure that all children receive both focused support and quality teacher time. For this to work, it depends not only on effective communication between the teacher and the other adults in the room but also on the TA being in the room and actively engaged in the support of learning throughout the lesson.

Key points to remember:

- TAs' support for learning needs to be active throughout the lesson, not just 'activated' during the individual or group learning.
- If a child cannot access the instructions, they will struggle with the learning task, so support for accessing instructions is vital.
- To promote inclusion, all the adults in the room need to work to promote children's independence. For most children, this can be done through small tweaks and adaptations, but these take time to implement and embed.

Things to discuss with senior leaders

- Consider the timing of interventions so that TAs are able to support the whole lesson and are not expected to be running interventions during key learning moments.
- If groups of children regularly leave the room for all or part of a lesson, are they being excluded from the learning? Instead, consider how they could be supported and included in the classroom at each phase of the lesson.

- What additional IT support/equipment is available for key children? This can be considered a 'reasonable adjustment' for a SEND child.

Things to think about

- What is the focus of the learning? Which activities will a child need to complete to demonstrate their understanding and which are administrative tasks that can be completed by someone else?
- What different options could we offer to support children to record independently? Do they need to write to show their learning?

Things that work really well

- Discuss the use of different resources in your classroom with your TA and your class at the beginning of the school year and at intervals throughout the year. It is very easy to assume adults know how to use cubes, Dienes, Numicon, number lines and other resources. They don't always, and might need to be shown and reminded.
- Build a bank of shared strategies your TA can use at each part of the lesson to support with specific examples.
- With a group of colleagues, 'brainstorm' as many different ways of recording and demonstrating learning as you can, then consider how many you can and do use.

6 Interventions

'It can be calmer outside the classroom, which can be good for small groups. I would like to see the group or the staff varied so all staff work with all children at some point in the week.'

TA

When children do not make the progress hoped for, we often look for 'interventions' to support them. However, we are not always clear what we mean by an intervention. Interventions should be about providing the right support at the right time. Despite it being common practice in many schools, this does not automatically mean an activity or group outside the classroom, with an additional adult. To be effective, interventions need to be relevant to and support the learning in the classroom. The majority of interventions are and should be small tweaks and adaptions within good, differentiated classroom practice, undertaken by you or your TA, or a combination of both, in the classroom.

Case study

In a Year 3 class there was a small group working very significantly below age expectations (still working on the Year 1 and EYFS curriculum). The class had a very strong TA. It quickly became daily practice that the TA took this group out of the main classroom each morning for literacy and maths and taught them in the nearby resource room. While the TA did her best to provide what the children needed, her curriculum was a haphazard mixture of attainment levels, content and guesswork based on the teacher's planning. To some extent it was a matter of out of sight, out of mind and

> the teacher lost sight of what these children were learning and how. The children made little progress and the gap between them and their peers increased.

In cases like this or where a child attends multiple short interventions, they can end up spending longer out of the class than in it. They can lose their sense of belonging and any real understanding of what they are learning. Their learning can become disjointed and constantly interrupted as they move from group to group.

At this point we move from interventions to 'outventions',[3] where the child is effectively excluded from the class. Often, rather than receiving quality-first teaching from a teacher, they get 'echo' teaching from a TA, often based on second-hand lesson plans or programmes, which the TA may have only received just before they delivered them. The current approach to phonics teaching, with its focus on regular group and one-to-one additional 'catch-up' sessions, is leading to an increasing number of interventions outside the classroom for an increasing range of children.

There are short interventions that may need to take place outside the classroom. These could include:

- occupational therapy, physio and other work to meet specific physical or sensory needs, though these can sometimes be included in PE lessons and movement breaks for the whole class
- speech and language work, though some of this could be included in phonic sessions
- SEMH and wellbeing interventions, such as ELSA, nurture and THRIVE
- very specific time-bound academic interventions focused on a particular learning skill, e.g. phonics catch-up.
- pre-learning, in which children are introduced to the vocabulary they will need to access the learning.

---

[3] I thank Ruth Swailes for the coining of this useful word.

Occasionally, there are children with significant SEND needs who require a completely differentiated curriculum. But this must be a conscious decision, not something that drifts into place. We need to ensure they continue to receive their entitlement to teacher time. There is a concern that the 'no excuses', one-size-fits-all agenda in education means that any child who cannot easily access the core teaching is effectively excluded and sent out to the care of a TA in an intervention group.

We tend to fall back on withdrawing children for interventions because it makes the impact easier to identify, measure and evidence. If a child is going out to 'a group', everyone – parents, child, SLT, those involved in the SEND system – can see the child is being supported, even if this is not the most appropriate support.

Additionally, a lot of TA deployment is based on 'what we have always done', including withdrawing children for a set 'menu' of interventions for which the school has the resources and/or for which staff have been trained. This often means that the child is fitted to the intervention rather than the intervention to the child.

Personal story

I visited a secondary school in which every child with a reading age below a certain level was withdrawn from lessons for 30 minutes twice a week to do a phonics-based reading intervention. They asked me to look at why this was not improving reading levels. It was clear that this was the wrong intervention for many of the children.

- *Many had failed to learn to read using phonics in primary school. Continuing to use the same approach was demoralising for the children. Why this had not worked for them earlier wasn't taken into account. They needed something different, not more of the same.*

- *Thirty minutes in one session was too long and twice a week was not enough. They needed more, but shorter, slots.*
- *Many of the children were being pulled out of lessons they liked in order to do something they found difficult, so they resented the intervention and did not fully engage.*
- *It was seen as something for 'thickos' and stigmatising by the children and some staff.*
- *The texts they were reading were frankly dull, not necessarily age-appropriate and nothing to do with the children's learning. Getting better at reading* The Three Billy Goats Gruff *does not help a child access a chemistry lesson!*

Yet this was what the school had always done and they struggled to imagine an alternative.

Linking interventions and classroom learning

The key to successful interventions is a clear linkage between the intervention and what is being taught in the classroom (EEF, 2021a). When these become separated, children are faced with two unrelated curriculums, meaning those with the most difficulties with generalising are being asked to create links between learning taught in different contexts.

Case study

In Year 4, Theo went out for a regular maths intervention, focusing on developing his number bond and times table recall. He really enjoyed the group and playing different

> games to support his number facts knowledge. He even tolerated the regular tests at the end of the sessions. He was excited to get certificates for his number bonds to ten and two times table facts. However, Theo, the TA and his teacher were increasingly frustrated that he was not able to reuse this knowledge in maths lessons. Eventually, Theo was able to explain that in the intervention group it looked different, 'it was fun' and the atmosphere was quiet.

We need to be very aware that there are many children who can access learning in a small group focused just on that area or skill but who continue to struggle to apply their learning in a whole class setting, with the extended language demands and hustle and bustle of the classroom. There need to be explicit connections between the learning in different settings to support children to transfer their skills between them.

Interventions in the room

Even when an intervention takes place within the classroom, there is still a risk of effective exclusion where a child becomes separated from the teacher (and often their peers) and is taught largely or even solely by a TA.

If this isn't working…	…try this
Mufasta had significant speech and language difficulties and an EHCP. He needed much of the language in the classroom to be simplified, and in Year 4 he needed work differentiated to Year 1 level. He tended to sit quietly at the back with his TA, who differentiated the learning for him.	The teacher moved Mufasta to sit at the front of the room with a small group of others who were also working below age expectations. In most lessons either she or the TA sat with this group and supported them with differentiated tasks. The teacher gained a better understanding of Mufasta's

His teacher realised that she knew little about Mufasta or what he was learning. He was very shy and she rarely spoke to him and he never spoke to her.	needs and he gained more confidence to engage with her. Increasingly, the teacher was able to set him short tasks that he could access independently and, using his pre-learning visual prompts, Mufasta began to be able to take part in whole class inputs.

By moving where Mufasta sat, his teacher broke the pattern in which the TA had become an intermediary between him and her, so Mufasta was able to access quality-first teaching first-hand. The most successful interventions take place through small tweaks and adaptations, rather than schemes and large actions.

Case study

Jonah was exceptionally able, but his high levels of anxiety meant that he was unable to engage in any writing task. He was frequently aggressive and was at risk of permanent exclusion. As he moved into Year 5, his teacher changed the approach to writing tasks for Jonah. At the beginning of the task, she would open his book, give him a pencil and then leave him either to write or not with no pressure. Slowly, with this low-pressure approach, he began to record a few words. Over the year, he wrote more. Although it was still not reflective of his ability, Jonah became more able to take part in lessons involving writing without distress or aggression.

Interventions outside the classroom

When we consider interventions outside the classroom, we need to be aware that 'outside' has many meanings. It can mean a specialised group room, sensory room, swimming pool, nurture farm or forest school area, but too often it means a space in a library, hall, corridor or even the cloakroom. An important issue for any intervention to be successful is an appropriate setting. Too often children with difficulties with focus and attention are taken out of class to try to learn in an area that is not comfortable, quiet or conducive to learning.

Equally we need to consider the length and frequency of interventions. EEF and MITA's research (2021) is clear that TA-led interventions can have a very positive impact, within certain conditions. They tell us that the best interventions involve the following conditions:

- They are often brief (20 to 50 minutes), occur regularly (three to five times per week) and are maintained over a sustained period (eight to 20 weeks).
- They are carefully timetabled so they are delivered consistently.
- The TAs receive extensive training from experienced trainers and/or teachers (five to 30 hours per intervention).
- The intervention has structured supporting resources and lesson plans, with clear objectives.
- The TAs follow the plan and structure of the intervention closely.
- Assessments are used to identify appropriate pupils, guide areas for focus and track pupil progress.
- Connections are made between the out-of-class learning in the intervention and the classroom (Sharples et al, 2018, p. 20).

The EEF points to a handful of interventions 'with a secure evidence base' (2021), which they identify as showing that targeted interventions, led by TAs, can demonstrate a consistent impact on attainment of approximately three to four additional months' progress. This is dependent on structured settings with high-quality support and training. Unfortunately, though these conditions are regularly aspired to, they are not always achieved.

If an intervention is to be successful and fulfil its objectives and targets, the person delivering it needs to understand the learning, purpose and nature of the intervention. If we send off a TA with just a group of children and the instruction to improve their spelling, we should not be surprised that it is not effective.

Interventions often fail because the TAs do not have the training or skills to deliver what is required. This can reinforce the vicious circle where interventions are selected on the basis of the skills and experience of the TAs instead of the needs of the children, as there is not the time or money to train the TA to deliver what is needed. This means that the interventions are not effective support for children's progress.

As classroom teachers, we need to be aware of the possible limitations of the interventions we plan and then make choices about the most appropriate support for our children on the basis of them.

Home-grown and evidence-based interventions

Many schools end up using 'home-grown' interventions or vaguely, but not strictly, following commercial or 'evidence-based' interventions.

'Home-grown' interventions		Commercial schemes	
Pros	Cons	Pros	Cons
• Easily adapted to the children's needs • Can respond directly to needs identified in the class • Useful for picking up and responding to misconceptions • Easier to make clear and direct links between the class learning and the intervention	• Requires skills and a real understanding of the curriculum to deliver effective interventions, which are often not present • Impact is difficult to assess • Tendency to drift • It takes time and effort to find the appropriate resources • Often ad hoc and ineffective	• Clear structure, aims and targets • Training and resources are often easily available • Clear entry and exit criteria • A clear evidence base so we know that they are effective • Support for TAs to develop skills and understanding • A clear script to support • Quick to set up	• We end up fitting the children to the intervention, even where it does not fit their needs • It is not delivered as it should be and its effectiveness is reduced • Often expensive • Schools use what they have, which may not be the same as what they need • Inflexible timing and approach • TAs pick them up without preparation • TAs don't follow the script • Not linked to the curriculum in the classroom

Interventions

Schools' variations and personalisations of evidence-based interventions or commercial schemes are not the same as the full scheme and will not have the same impact. However, they may work better or be the only feasible way of working in our settings.

> 'There are real issues with scripted interventions when the script doesn't fit the children. Too many interventions do not fit the needs of the children, or the TA lacks the skills, knowledge and confidence to make it fit, as they are scared to deviated from the script.'
>
> Headteacher

Making interventions work

Clearly, what makes an intervention work and worthwhile depends on what you want it to achieve. EEF looks at three to four months' additional progress (2021b). Others look for greater levels of progress. Some will accept less progress, provided that there are gains in other areas, such as pupil confidence or engagement. Equally, not all interventions have purely academic objectives: some may be focused on wellbeing, SEMH needs, physical or communication skills.

To know whether an intervention has a positive impact, you do need some form of entry and exit data and targets. This is clear with an intervention focused on clear academic targets, like the recall and use of times tables, but more difficult with less academically based interventions, though things such as pupil confidence scales can help. There is a further issue when children can do things in intervention groups, but not apply the skills in the classroom, as with Theo in the case study on page 136.

Managing practical issues: When? Where?

One of the ongoing issues of making interventions work is timetabling and ensuring that the interventions actually happen. They are all too often lost or allowed to slip so that their time is reduced. There is no easy answer to this, but it is worth considering what is realistic for your class and TA so that you focus on the times when things are less likely to be missed, e.g. not scheduling interventions immediately after lunch when your TA is regularly distracted by first aid or behaviour incidents.

To avoid impacting on other learning, interventions often take place at 'non-learning' times: lunchtime, register time, assembly, before or after school, 'even modern foreign language lessons' (Skipp and Hopwood, 2019). While accepting that a withdrawal group will require a child to miss some part of the curriculum or school day, it is important that we do not exclude them from the wider curriculum, particularly as for many these are the areas where they have a chance to shine and really enjoy learning.

Case study

Tilly struggled in all areas of the curriculum, except dance. She had always had good school attendance and tried hard in school. Suddenly, she started refusing to come to school and when she did arrive, she made only half-hearted attempts to engage with learning. It was only as the rest of the class changed for PE (a dance lesson) and Tilly was collected for yet another literacy intervention did her teacher identify the issue: Tilly felt that she was being punished for her learning difficulties by being made to miss the one thing she was really good at and enjoyed.

Often the timing of interventions can seem punitive to the children and give implicit messages about the importance of the wider curriculum. Further, there are risks that when children are withdrawn from PSHE (personal, social, health and economic education) and RSE (relationships and sex education) lessons, the children with the greatest need for the safeguarding messages delivered within these sessions may miss them.

We have already considered the difficult question of where interventions should take place. There is an additional issue that even when an appropriate place is found, this can often be impacted by other events in school, e.g. assessment week, visiting theatre groups and special assemblies, so sessions are missed. There are no easy answers to this, but it is important we don't end up running so many interventions that we give them no chance to be successful due to issues with timing or location.

Flipping the support

It is interesting that the EEF's work on intervention groups refers to them being run by teachers or TAs, yet they are almost always run by TAs (2018). It is worth considering that you could lead an intervention while your TA covers the class. Similarly, with interventions within the class, you could work with a small group, while your TA undertakes the roving role within the class.

Working with outside agencies

In many schools, there are a number of interventions (particularly, though not exclusively, for those with SEND) that are run under the direction, supervision or with the support of outside agencies or specialists, e.g. speech and language therapy, occupational and physical therapy, emotional and mental health support and EAL support. This work is often a key part of a child's SEND support and may be written in as a statutory requirement in their EHCP. This is often very successful and provides good support for the child and excellent professional development for the members of staff concerned. However, too often it is less than effective, as there is a lack of continuity for the members of staff involved or the intervention is not given priority when the specialist is not in school.

TAs as experts working across the school

Often where TAs have been trained in a particular intervention (Every Child Counts, ELSA, Read Write Inc, etc.), approach (nurture groups or forest school) or area (speech and language or phonic support), schools will deploy them to work and provide interventions in that area across the school. While this enables those staff to develop confidence and expertise, it can make liaison with class teachers and creating explicit links to the curriculum more difficult. There can also be issues of:

- fidelity to the programme
- teachers understanding the interventions – how they work and what they offer
- the intervention taking place – too often things slip due to TAs being redeployed, which means that the TAs and the children are given a message that they and their work are not important
- children's absence.

Pre- and over-learning: an example of a workable small-scale intervention

The idea of pre-learning is to give children the language to enable them to 'tune in' to learning. If we lack, do not understand or cannot access the language needed to understand what is going on, it is very hard to follow a conversation, text or piece of learning. Yet this is often what happens to children. Using pre-learning, children are explicitly taught the key vocabulary and concepts needed to follow, understand and engage in learning in a particular lesson. Additionally, pre-learning can:

- set the context for learning
- generate interest
- activate their previous learning

- support the acquisition of vocabulary and knowledge
- allow children to predict the content of lessons.

There are different elements in learning vocabulary, and pre-learning aims to activate them all.

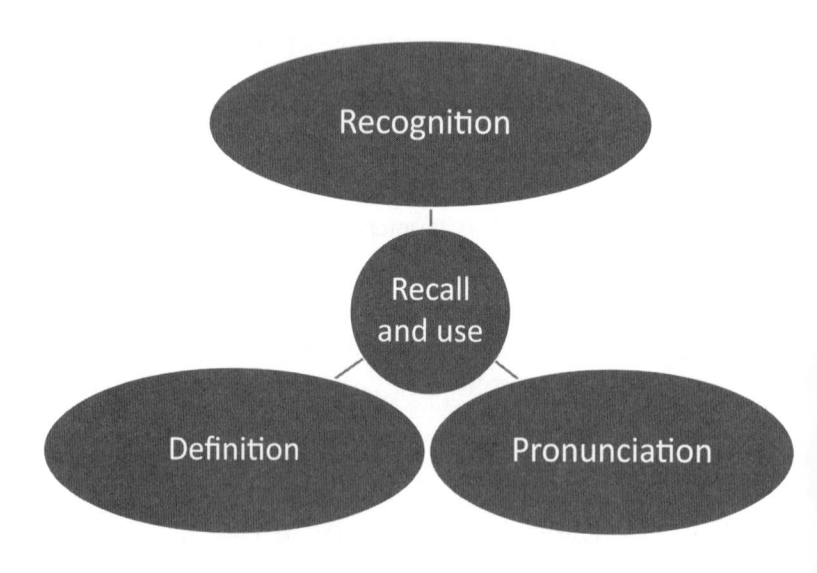

```
        Recognition
             |
        Recall
        and use
       /        \
  Definition   Pronunciation
```

- <u>Recognition:</u> How is the word spelled? The ability to use phonics to decode new vocabulary and then to spell it is important and enables a child to use the word in writing. However, many people can recognise words, even spell them, but do not understand or use them correctly.
- <u>Pronunciation:</u> How is the word said? Supporting children to say a word aloud and use it in sentences and context increases the likelihood that they will remember it. However, being able to read and say a word does not mean that you understand it.
- <u>Definition:</u> What does the word mean? If you know the meaning of a word, you are much more likely to remember it. However, to use it, you need to be able to say, read and spell the word.

- <u>Recall and use:</u> To truly know and understand a word, a child needs to be able to apply their word knowledge in a range of contexts.

In addition to technical vocabulary, there are many words that are common in written text, but not so common in spoken language. It is these words that are key to understanding text, and the inability to understand them often makes reading texts difficult and frustrating, so children don't want to engage with them. Further, children are often confused by words with multiple, and often very different, meanings.

Pre-learning works by introducing children to a few (up to three) pieces of vocabulary before a lesson and ensuring that they understand them. This is usually supported by visual prompts so that they can recall and use the language during the lesson and engage when others do so.

Over-learning supports children to remember and continue to access their learning. It is a focused opportunity to:

- embed new vocabulary
- pick up and challenge misconceptions
- celebrate children using their new vocabulary
- enable children to make links to previous and next steps in learning.

Conclusion

Interventions out of the classroom are often seen as a clear response to show that we are doing something to support a child and meet their needs. Often when an intervention is separated from quality-first teaching within the classroom, it is easier to measure its impact. However, interventions need to be fit for purpose, and there is often a separation between class learning and the interventions that are supposed to support it. Successful interventions, both within and outside the classroom, should reflect children's learning needs and be delivered by trained staff. Moreover, we need to ensure that children are accessing both teacher time and TA support. It is often through small tweaks and adaptations in differentiated teaching that we make our most successful interventions.

Key points to remember:

- The choice of interventions should be about the needs of the children and not what we have always done or usually do.
- There is a danger that we are asking the most vulnerable children to do the most work to link their learning experiences between different settings.
- There is also a danger that inappropriate or poorly planned interventions become a form of exclusion.
- Poorly planned deployment of TAs can inhibit rather than promote children's progress, so it is important all TA-led interventions are consistent, directed towards children's needs, link with their learning in class and are delivered by well-trained staff.
- Not all interventions have to take place outside the classroom.

Things to discuss with senior leaders

- How have TAs been trained to lead interventions, particularly outside the classroom?
- Can you flip the support, so you lead the intervention and the TA takes the class?
- Are there set interventions your school always uses? Why is that? Is it possible to change the interventions the school uses?
- How quickly after the beginning of the school year should interventions be set up? How do you balance the need not

to waste time with the need to develop an understanding of children's needs and ensure their sense of belonging to a class group before you start an intervention?

Things to think about

- Do you know what is taught in the interventions the children in your class attend?
- If children have not managed to develop a key learning skill or knowledge after three or more years of using the same approach (e.g. reading using a phonics-based approach), should we continue with that approach or should we try something different or additional to promote their learning?
- Does the language we use to describe interventions to children make them feel punitive or stigmatising?
- How far can you provide interventions within your classroom through small tweaks and adaptations?

Things that work really well

- Take a register for all interventions; if a child consistently misses an intervention, it will reduce its impact.
- Use an intervention monitoring form to check progress against targets and record entry and exit assessments. An example can be found on the following pages.

Working Effectively With Your Teaching Assistant

Intervention	
TA/teacher responsible	
Year group	
Timing and frequency	
Children	Agreed targets
	1.
	2.
	3.

Week commencing	Group completed?	Observations and notes	Absent children

150

Evaluation of intervention

Children	Evaluation Target 1			Evaluation Target 2			Evaluation Target 3		
	Exceeded/Met/Not met			Exceeded/Met/Not met			Exceeded/Met/Not met		
	Exceeded/Met/Not met			Exceeded/Met/Not met			Exceeded/Met/Not met		
	Exceeded/Met/Not met			Exceeded/Met/Not met			Exceeded/Met/Not met		
	Exceeded/Met/Not met			Exceeded/Met/Not met			Exceeded/Met/Not met		
	Exceeded/Met/Not met			Exceeded/Met/Not met			Exceeded/Met/Not met		
	Exceeded/Met/Not met			Exceeded/Met/Not met			Exceeded/Met/Not met		
	Exceeded/Met/Not met			Exceeded/Met/Not met			Exceeded/Met/Not met		
Effectiveness of group	% Ex	% Met	% Not	% Ex	% Met	% Not	% Ex	% Met	% Not
Actions/next steps										

Interventions

7 Sharing planning and feedback

'We want to and do make a huge difference. Engage with us right from the planning stage and we will show you that we can help everyone fly.'

TA

If we are going to work effectively with our TAs, we need to try to get the communication right. Despite huge amounts of research and everyone's best intentions, the reality in many schools is that the TAs arrive with the children, receive little training and are expected to 'wing it' in the classroom. There are no magic answers to this, but there are lots of ways of making it easier.

In 2019, the DfE recognised the importance of planning time for TAs. However, it was only for HLTAs and those with additional qualifications, when they are providing interventions or tasks with a 'higher level of skill or responsibility', e.g. covering classes (Skipp and Hopwood, 2019 p. 24). It was also not clear what was meant by 'planning time' and they admitted that it might be no more than a quick informal conversation. The result is that often schools depend on the personal relationships between teachers and TAs and on a shared commitment to going above and beyond to ensure effective communication in the classroom. This should not be the basis of our working practices, nor should there be an expectation that we will form a close friendship with our TA, so we need strategies to make those conversations effective, regardless of our relationship.

Making time to communicate

Finding time to communicate can be a huge challenge. This can mean that when you do talk, the communication is often very superficial. While issuing directions and giving instructions are vital for making your class run smoothly, if this is your only communication with your TA, it is hard to form an effective relationship and there is a risk that all your communications will fail.

> 'Time chatting with your TA can feel like time wasted, but it is a vital part of your relationship, which is part of how you support the children in your class.'
>
> Teacher

There is a clear balance that needs to be struck. If your only communication with your TA is gossip about the headteacher's cat, that will not support learning. But remembering that you are both people and trying to understand what makes you both tick will. Further, the modelling of effective, friendly and professional relationships is in itself important learning for the children.

Having established that our communication needs to be more than just the delivery of instructions (and gossip), we need to consider what should be included in effective communication with our TAs:

- An understanding of the children, their needs and barriers to learning, but **also** their strengths and motivators. Too often our communication with our TAs becomes focused solely on what the children can't do, so we forget to share their successes.

- What we are going to teach, why and how. Sadly, the 'what' often overshadows the 'why' and 'how'. As with the children, your TA needs to share the learning journey and context of the learning for it to make sense.

- The content of a particular lesson and what the TA needs to do to support learning. This may include who they are going to work with, though this may need to be flexible within the lesson.
- The strategies and approaches you are going to use or want the TA to use to support learning for the whole class or individuals.
- Feedback about how the learning went. This is key for assessment and planning next steps.

Implicit within this is an understanding of our communication with TAs as a two-way process. We can get so caught up with what we need to tell our TA that we forget to listen. TAs will have important information about children and their learning to impart. They will have questions to ask about the learning and lesson process. If they are struggling to follow it, the children may also struggle.

If this isn't working…	…try this
As a trainee teacher, Anne was receiving repeated feedback that her explanations were too long and confused. She was getting very disheartened and was about to give up.	At this moment Bethan, the TA in her class, stepped in. She gently said that she sometimes struggled to follow the explanations and suggested that Anne practised them on her. As Anne stumbled through the explanations, Bethan was able to ask questions and suggest clarifications. The whole process meant that Anne was able to develop her ideas more clearly and realise when she was assuming knowledge that wasn't there.

We know that interventions are less effective when they do not link to what is happening in the classroom. So it is vital, if TAs are running interventions or other support activities outside the classroom, that they give us feedback about them so that they can be linked to what is happening in the classroom. Also, TAs often have information about children's interactions in the playground, and occasionally beyond the school gate, which is key for us to understand fully what is going on for the children.

> 'Ask our opinions – we sometimes spend longer talking to the children, at playtime for instance, so may have different ideas of what motivates them.'
>
> TA

Developing a shared language and understanding of learning

For teachers and TAs to work well together, it is fundamental that they have a shared language and understanding of the learning.

Case study

Stephano had an EHCP and was working within the Year 1 curriculum in Year 3. The class teacher and SENCo agreed that the key strategy to support his writing was that he should verbalise his sentences several times, setting out a cube for each word and then a dice to represent the full stop. He then used this to support him to recall and record the sentence.

Both the teacher and SENCo were clear that Stephano should not be dictating sentences that were recorded before he copied them into his book. This was included on his individual support plan and discussed regularly with Sarah-Jane, the class TA.

However, each day Sarah-Jane started with her preferred strategy (dictation and copying) and each day the teacher had to remind her of the agreed plan and model the strategies. It

> was not that Sarah-Jane did not remember or understand the plan; it was that she felt that the suggested strategies took too long and stopped her helping others.
>
> It was only after considerable discussion, and the intervention of both the SENCo and headteacher, that Sarah-Jane began to accept that her focus on copying hindered the development of Stephano's writing skills and his independence, and left him confused as he could not predict what strategies he would be expected to use.

A shared understanding may take time to develop. It is all too easy to forget what we know and have learned in our training as teachers; we sometimes take it for granted and assume that it is obvious. While some TAs are very experienced and some have benefited from significant training, many are/have not. They are working on what they have picked up as they have gone along, and this may include some fundamental misconceptions. We must not assume understanding on either side. This includes the 'why' as well as the 'what' of our lessons.

When we are planning a lesson, we go through a process that includes:

- checking our subject knowledge
- planning the lesson, including how it fits with the previous and next steps of learning
- gathering resources
- considering support, stretch and challenge for different pupils.

In an ideal world, we would give our TAs the opportunity and support to do the same.

Sharing planning

One TA summed up the issues of sharing planning:

> 'We didn't plan it, it's not as obvious to us!'

For TAs to be able to follow our planning, they need to be able to see, share and understand it. This includes being given time to read it. If TAs (and teachers) are not prepared, it impacts the effectiveness of their work.

Why we need to share planning	What happens if we don't
To support and promote children's independence and give them opportunities to take risks with their learning.	TAs tend to fall back on over-prompting and spoon feeding children the answers.
To provide children with appropriate visuals to support their understanding and vocabulary, staff need to know both what is coming up and what the key vocabulary is.	The visuals are often haphazard, inappropriate or introduced at the wrong time.
To ensure that a TA can support children to focus on the learning.	If a TA is not confident with what the learning is, it can be difficult for them to separate it from the administration. Then they may focus on that and on task completion, rather than on learning.

Why we need to share planning	What happens if we don't
To enable TAs to support children with clear instructions.	If TAs are not sure what is happening in a lesson, they tend to engage in stereo teaching: repeating your instructions and often adding to children's confusion, rather than effectively prompting them for learning or engagement.
To support TAs to use effective questioning to promote learning and extend thinking.	TAs tend to use questions just to check the recall of facts.

The reality is that TAs rarely have time to be involved directly in the planning process, so their involvement tends to be reactive rather than proactive – commenting on and asking questions about what has been shared with them, rather than contributing at the planning creation stage.

What to share

For most teachers, their planning is a multi-layer document, including long-term, medium-term and short-term planning. Often it is only the short-term planning that gets shared with TAs. If the other layers of planning are shared, they are rarely explained. However, the long- and medium-term planning are part of the big picture of what we are teaching and why. This can be one of the classic occasions when teachers assume understanding. By sharing the long- and medium-term planning, we support our TAs to understand what is coming up and how it fits with what we are teaching now and taught in the past.

How to share planning

Many schools say that planning is available for all staff, and often that it is on 'the system' and they just need to log in. This is easier said than done. Few TAs have the time during the school day to log onto the school server, find the planning and then read, process and absorb it. In addition to the implicit and unfair expectation that they should log in outside their working hours, there are some TAs who struggle with the technical skills and device access to do this at home.

Many teachers do their planning through their teaching slides. It is helpful for your TA to see the slides in advance and even more helpful if they are annotated with what you want your TA to know about the learning and the practical aspects of the lesson, e.g. which groups you want them to work with.

If this isn't working…	…try this
Marina shared the link to her planning each Sunday evening with her TA, Laila. But each week, she became more and more frustrated when Laila hadn't read the planning and was not clear on what she needed to do or why. The deputy head mediated a conversation between them. Laila explained that on a Sunday evening she had to put her children to bed and prepare their school lunches and school bags before sorting herself out for work. She did not have time to read the planning. Further, the only device she had for reading it on was her phone and she found it really hard to read on that.	Marina realised that it was not fair to ask Laila to read the planning in her own time, particularly not on a Sunday evening. So she changed her way of working, so that she gave Laila a printed version of the planning when she came in on a Monday morning. Then while Marina did the register and Monday morning tables test, Laila could go through the planning. Marina highlighted what she wanted Laila to do, so that it was quicker for her to refer to in the lesson.

Making it work using just three questions

To get the basic communications about planning down to a useful minimum, I use three key questions. These will fit on a large sticky note!

What is the learning intention?	Different schools describe these differently, but it is what the children are going to be learning, i.e. the focus of the lesson. This needs to include enough information to be useful, e.g. not just 'addition' but 'addition with exchange using formal methods with two- and three-digit numbers'.
What is the key vocabulary?	What new, technical or unusual vocabulary will the children need in order to access learning? It is really helpful to highlight the vocabulary on your planning and/or slides. What are the words that children may not know or remember? Also, what is the key vocabulary they will need to access the learning? These are the words the TA could use as prompts with the children. If you are using pre-learning (see page 145), this vocabulary should be the focus of that intervention.
What is the outcome?	What are the children expected to produce by the end of the lesson? Consider what flexibility there is in this, so the task can be adapted to meet children's needs and different ways of demonstrating their learning. Use this to support your TAs to focus on the learning, not just task completion.

> ### Case study
>
> Rachel was a very experienced TA. She liked to use the three questions to help her plan how she would work with children with SEND. In one lesson, she saw that the learning intention was to write a poem about autumn using rhyming couplets. The second question made it clear that the key vocabulary for the lesson was about the structure of poems (rhyme, couplet, verse, line, stanza) and the outcome was to write a poem including rhyming couplets.
>
> Rachel was working with Willow. She knew that Willow would struggle to write about autumn but would be more confident writing about her guinea pig. She checked in with the teacher and then changed the task for Willow, so she still met the learning intention, used the key vocabulary and produced something appropriate to the lesson outcome, but in a context that worked for her.
>
> Equally, if the focus of the lesson had been developing understanding about autumn, it might have been appropriate for Willow to produce a non-fiction piece of writing or a story board or annotate a picture, rather than write a poem.

Tackling the issue of subject knowledge

As teachers, we get a considerable amount of training and have degree-level education. We have a specialism in a particular area and we may have years of classroom experience. Even so, sometimes we have to take time to research what we are teaching. It is not surprising that many TAs do not have the same level of subject knowledge. Even where they do have the subject knowledge, the way we teach maths and English, particularly phonics, has changed dramatically in the last ten years. We cannot and should not assume that TAs have the subject knowledge to support their teaching.

The more difficult question is what we do about this. Ideally, TAs would receive training to build their subject knowledge, but we know that this is not always available or possible. So we need to recognise that this is an issue and find ways of working around it, including:

- Looking ahead at your long- and medium-term planning with your TA and having honest discussions about where they (and you) feel less confident, so that you have time to plug the gaps.
- Working with other teachers and TAs in your year group or beyond to have 'mini tutorials' and teach each other. This is great practice to fine-tune your explanations so that they are clear for the children.
- Using the time in the lesson to model learning together. It is a great opportunity to model the fact that you and your TA don't know everything and that it is safe to make mistakes.
- Making time and ensuring that it feels safe for your TA to ask questions. Even when TAs do have the subject knowledge, they may not be confident about it.

If this isn't working…	…try this
Although Rob and Gurpreet were working well together and the children were learning and making progress, they were getting increasingly stressed with each other.	The following week Rob tried to take more time to go through the week's lesson plans and at each point he stressed to Gurpreet that she knew about the learning and he mentioned what a good job she had done with this group or in this area the previous week.
Gurpreet was heard in the staff room complaining that Rob never gave her any direction; he just gave her the lesson plans and left her to get on with it.	At this point, she turned to him with a big smile and said, 'So you think I am doing a good job!'
Rob was getting irritated that Gurpreet seemed to always be wanting him to go over the lesson plans multiple times, which felt to him like a waste of time as she knew perfectly well what to do.	Rob's response was to look confused and say, 'Of course.' This was all Gurpreet needed: the confirmation that she was doing the right thing in the right way. She couldn't know unless she was told.

Top tips for sharing planning

- Provide a printed copy of the planning, then your TA can make notes on it.
- Highlight what you want your TA to do. Depending on their experience and confidence with the curriculum, this might be just including their initials or it may need to be more detailed information.
- If you are sharing slides as planning, consider whether there is enough information included to make your thinking clear; if not, add notes.
- Include what resources will be needed to support learning.
- Check with your TA when it is most helpful for them to receive the planning. This will vary from person to person.

Completing the circle: Feedback

Learning from Early Years

In giving feedback about children, as in so many things, we can learn from our Early Years colleagues. In EYFS, making observations is a key part of the information-gathering and evidence about children's learning. All the adults in the room can and should make observations to contribute to the learning journey. This culture of thinking about what children are doing and learning as part of daily practice is not always present as we move up the school.

As teachers, we cannot be everywhere and we need observations from our TAs, particularly when they are working directly with individuals or groups, to add to our understanding of the children's learning. The key question is how to make the process of sharing feedback effective and manageable. This has to be part of the two-way communication process with our TAs.

Identifying the level of support

It is key to understand the level of support that a child needs to access and engage in a particular task. If we are not there, this is not always clear from the outcome. There is a huge difference in learning between a child who wrote a piece entirely independently and a child who orally rehearsed with prompting and was then supported to write each line, yet the outcome may look the same. A starting point for feedback is an indicator of the level of support. Often this can be a code written in the child's book, e.g.:

I = independent

IS = initial support

S = supported

There are many more examples of such codes, and these will depend on what works for you and your TA and the school marking policy.

When we need more detail

Some schools actively encourage 'live marking' within the lesson and promote TA involvement in it; others do not. You have to work within your school's policy. Even where a TA has written a comment in a child's book, it does not always provide you with the information that you need to understand how the child approached and responded to the learning.

Equally, it is not sensible or practical to ask your TA to write long comments in children's books or elsewhere. Some teachers and TAs find a simple feedback form works better when the TA is working with a single child or small group, for example:

Lesson:	Date:
Child's name	Comment

Alternatively, your TA can write short comments on sticky notes, which can either be stuck onto the children's book and removed once read or stuck onto a copy of the planning. You can then use the information to feed into planning future lessons, or even into reports and parents' evening information.

Whatever the format, it is worth considering and discussing with your TA what is and is not useful feedback to ensure that your TA spends more time supporting children than writing about how they supported them.

Useful feedback	Less useful feedback
How a group of children worked together Why: This tells you about the children's learning behaviour, and how they approached the learning and shared the task.	**How many spellings a child got wrong in a general class piece of writing** Why: You can see this quickly for yourself and it adds little to your understanding of the child's difficulties. It is better if the TA can explain the strategies the child was using for spelling and whether there were any patterns in the words they got right or wrong.
About a sudden change in a child's behaviour or attitude Why: We communicate through our behaviour. A sudden change in behaviour suggests the child is bothered by something. It could be an indicator of a safeguarding concern.	**A child has completed a task** Why: This does not add to your understanding of the child's learning. It is better for the TA to focus on what the child learned. What could they do or what did they know/were able to do at the end of the session that they didn't know/couldn't do at the beginning?

Useful feedback	Less useful feedback
When a child approached a task in an unusual or interesting way Why: This gives an insight into the child's learning and understanding.	**A child has done well or enjoyed an activity** Why: This information alone doesn't identify what the child has done or learned or what strategies they used. We need more detail to understand and plan for the next step in their learning.
When a child unexpectedly struggled with something or exceeded expectations Why: As adults in the classroom, we have expectations of the children. When they don't meet them, we need to consider why and how to respond.	**The child has read pages 3–12** Why: While it might be useful to know what page a child is on, what is really useful is to know how they read.

If your TA is marking spellings, tables tests, etc., while it is important to note the score, the key information is not necessarily about the children who got most of the questions right (they had learned the material effectively or already knew it) or wrong (the test was not appropriate for them or they hadn't learned the material), but those who regularly get about a third wrong. This suggests difficulties with their strategies for learning and recalling the information or, if there are patterns across several children, that the way the material is taught needs to be reconsidered.

The information from our TAs should feed into the Assess, Plan, Do, Review cycle that underlies our teaching. Our planning needs to be fluid to respond to different needs. There is no point in moving onto the next stage of planning if children have not understood the previous stage.

Working with children with SEND

When they are working with children with SEND, it is particularly important that your TA not only shares feedback on the child's learning, approach and wellbeing, but that this is also fed back into their support plan and individual targets.

> **Case study**
>
> Meg was the key person for Milah, who had significant special needs. She kept a copy of his support plan and targets in a file, which could be accessed by anyone who worked with Milah. She wrote regular notes in it against each target and encouraged everyone else working with him, including the teacher, to do the same. This meant that there was consistency in the approaches being used and staff were able to build on Milah's previous learning effectively. When it was time to review his targets with the SENCo and his parents, the teacher was able to check and share his progress immediately and accurately.

Conclusion

Sharing of planning and feedback is key to recognising and allowing TAs to demonstrate their professionalism. It is important to find a way to communicate that works for you and your TA. Many classrooms have teacher/TA communication books, but these often focus on admin tasks. While this is important, our focus needs to be on children's learning and wellbeing.

Like teachers, TAs have a role both before and after the learning takes place. They need to be given time to fulfil these roles. This depends on effective communication, which is not easy. We need to recognise its importance and not believe that somehow communication will fit in by magic. We actually need to make time for it, such as setting a time for sharing planning at least once a week and sticking to it, and building regular feedback into our daily routine.

We need to be aware of how we communicate in front of children. The reality is that much of teacher/TA communication is a quick conversation, often grabbed over the children's heads. We need to be aware of the language we use, as children will hear and it will impact on them and their responses, engagement and self-esteem. This includes unspoken communications: children see and feel eye rolls, smirks and pitying smiles. The interactions of the adults in classrooms are a model for the children's communications and working relationships. Our communication should always be professional.

Key points to remember:

- All the documents we use for communication need to be working documents that you and the TA(s) can add to and share.
- Staff need to be alerted to changes in the plans.
- Don't assume that TAs know and understand what you know. Take the time to explain.
- Ensure that your TA has time to read planning and that it is presented in a way that is accessible for them.
- TAs should spend more time supporting children than writing about how they supported them.

Things to discuss with senior leaders

- How do you ensure that you keep personal information about children secure?
- What are their ideas about sharing information with support staff? How and when is time given to do this? Is it possible for your TA to join you for some of your PPA time to share planning?

Things to think about

- What works as a way of communication for the staff working in your room to share planning? Is this different for different people?
- How do you balance the sharing of information about a particular lesson and the understanding of skills development and subject knowledge?
- What information does your TA have to share with you, as well as what you need to tell them?

Things that work really well

- Develop a planning folder that your TAs can dip into, which includes long-term and medium-term planning as well as short-term planning, so that they can see the whole learning journey.
- Use the pupil profile included in Chapter 2 to identify and share children's strengths and motivators, as well as their barriers to learning and the strategies to support them, on one page.

8 Supporting with behaviour: consistency imbued with flexibility

'Sharing and discussing our expectations means we provide a united front. The children feel safe, learn and behave better.'

Teacher

Support for learning needs to be more than just supporting the academic side of things. Support for wellbeing, behaviour and learning needs to be intrinsically linked. However, in many classes TAs focus chiefly on supporting behaviour. This reflects not only the needs of individual children, but also the difficulties of teaching others when there is disruptive behaviour from one or more children. However, children's behaviour cannot be seen in isolation. It needs to be understood as a form of communication. If we focus solely on behaviour management, this quickly becomes separated from meaningful support for learning.

You and your TA need to work together to understand children's behaviour and what they are trying to communicate. Whatever a child's special needs or diagnosis, their needs are likely to be reflected in their communications and social interactions, focus, coordination and sensory needs, which will in turn impact their understanding, learning, processing and behaviour. Equally, we should not assume that because a child is 'behaving' they are learning. A child who is withdrawn should be as much of a concern as a child who is 'acting out'. A child with a high level of anxiety or whose focus is fully taken up with trying to regulate their emotions will struggle with learning as much as one who is engaged in large, disruptive behaviours.

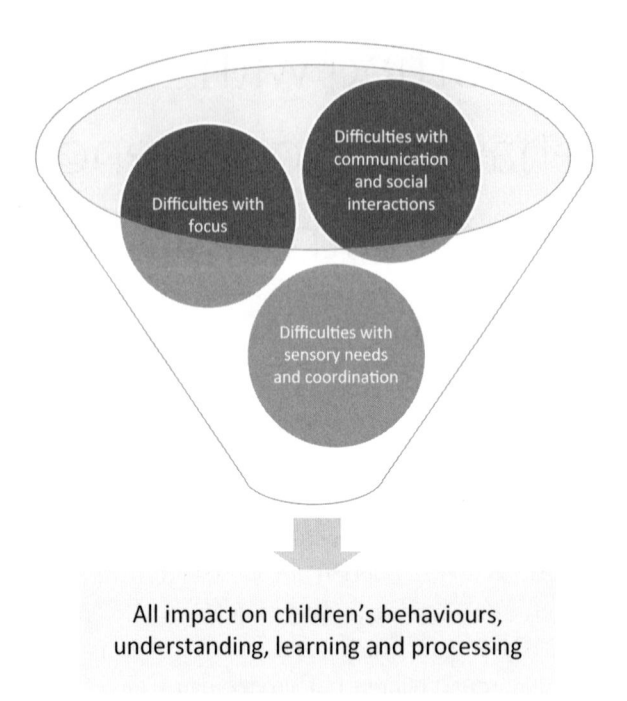

```
         ┌─────────────────────────────────┐
          ╲  ┌─────────┐  ┌──────────────┐ ╱
           ╲ │Difficulties│ │Difficulties with│╱
            ╲│ with focus │ │ communication │
             │           │ │ and social    │
              ╲          ╱ │ interactions  │
               ╲        ╱  └──────────────┘
                ╲  ┌──────────────┐  ╱
                 ╲ │Difficulties with│ ╱
                  ╲│ sensory needs  │╱
                   │and coordination│
                    ╲              ╱
                     ╲            ╱
                      ╲          ╱
                       ╲        ╱
                        ▼      ▼
```

All impact on children's behaviours, understanding, learning and processing

Leading on behaviour in your classroom

As the teacher, you need to lead on behaviour in your classroom and avoid devolving it to your TA. To do this effectively, you need to be clear about your roles and work to maintain a positive relationship with every child (and each other). Often classroom staff can fall into the good cop/bad cop model, where one enforces discipline and the other deals with problems. This can lead to children feeling insecure and uncertain of boundaries. Some will then need to test the boundaries to try to understand the rules and how they work.

If this isn't working…	…try this
Vernon was adopted from care and struggled to regulate his emotions. He had a sixth sense for any discrepancies in messages about what he was expected to do and would test these to the limit. When Vernon picked up on any differences between the teacher and TA, he would then go from one to the other asking the same question and becoming more anxious about the responses, until he became distraught and the head would need to be called to remove him from the room.	It was recognised that Vernon needed consistency and to be certain that all the adults around him were in agreement. His teacher and TA worked very hard to present information to him in the same way, but they also agreed that when he questioned things, the TA would always say 'I think…, but shall we go and check with Ms Brown [the teacher]?' While this took time, it ensured that the message was consistent and Vernon could see that both adults were in agreement. This reduced his anxiety and increased his ability to regulate his emotions and stay in the classroom.

Listening to the communications

Often, we and our TA respond directly to visible behaviours – fidgeting, talking, low-level disruption, 'rudeness' and aggression, etc. – without considering what is going on for the child that is leading to these behaviours. This makes it harder to support either behaviour or learning.

The 'iceberg model' can help to focus discussions between you and your TA, helping you identify:

- children's presenting, visual behaviours
- children's underlying needs, difficulties and unvoiced communications
- strategies that work to support them.

[Diagram: an iceberg with "Visible behaviours" above the waterline and "Underlying needs, difficulties and unvoiced communications" below, with "Supportive strategies" shown alongside, connected by arrows.]

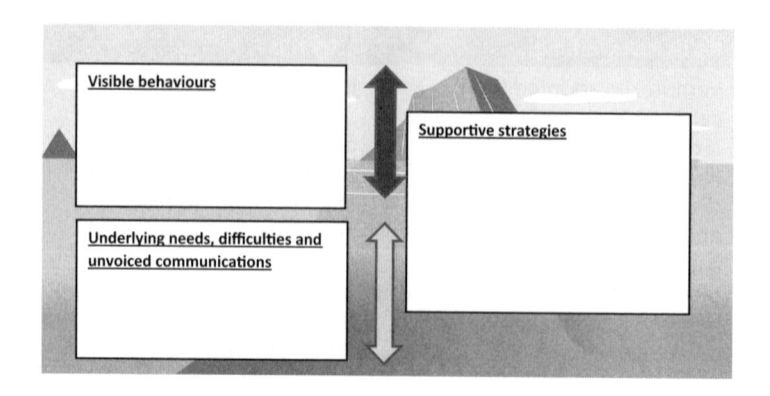

Many of the strategies that we can use to support children's behaviour are the same or similar to the ones we have looked at to support learning in previous chapters.

Underlying needs, difficulties and unvoiced communications	Why?	Possible supportive strategies
Difficulties managing change, transitions and routines	If we don't know what is going on, we become anxious and struggle to regulate our emotions. There are many children who struggle with change and/or who are very routine-bound. It helps them to manage this and to access learning if we are clear on what is happening and what is going to happen next.	• Visual timetables. • 'Now and next' boards. • 'If…then…' boards. These are another version of now and next boards: *If you do this* (the activity that the adult wants the child to engage with), *then* (the child can do a motivating activity or one of their choice). These work particularly well for children who feel that they need to remain in control of a situation.

			• Checklists for particular times of day, such as transitions, stating what children need at the beginning or end of the day, to go to a particular lesson or to start a task.
Difficulties with focus		Being able to focus in order to understand and follow instructions is key for a child to engage in learning.	• Pre-learning: if the child knows the language and context of what is being taught, it is easier for them to focus and follow. • Visual prompts for vocabulary. • Visual prompts as behaviour reminders. These enable your TA to support a child's focus without disrupting the lesson themselves. • Visual prompts to guide the child through the stages of the lesson. • A print-out of the teaching slides, so the child can track what is being said and avoid trying to access information at a distance. • Giving the child an individual whiteboard so that they can make notes – this can support focus and act as a fiddle object. • Fiddle objects – these are supports for learning and focus, not playthings.

Managing anxiety	Children often need time to calm so that they can access learning, and this can be supported by specific activities and the use of consistent language about them.	• Calm time: time out with a 'calming' and often repetitive activity, e.g. colouring, sewing or reading. • Calm boxes: boxes of activities for individuals or for a whole class. • Movement breaks: a structured break that supports a child to refocus and ground themselves through physical activity. • Sensory circuits: a daily intervention using a set of activities to meet different sensory needs to support self-regulation and preparation for learning.

For any of these strategies to work, we need clear agreement with our TA about how and when they will be implemented.

If this isn't working…	…try this
Poppy had a diagnosis of ASD (autism spectrum disorder). She struggled with anxiety. She had a box of calming activities that she could access when needed in the corner of the class. For a while this worked well: Poppy used her calm box and then returned to learning. However, as her anxieties about transitions increased, she struggled more and more to transition from her calming activities back to learning.	Melissa, the class TA, discussed the issue with the teacher and the SENCo. Together, they set up a Social Story™ reminding Poppy about the rules for her calm box. They set up a system so that Poppy could choose how long she would need to calm (a three- or five-minute slot) with a timer. At the end of this, Melissa would help her pack up her calm box and re-engage with learning. It didn't always work, but it helped.

> **EXTRA USEFUL INFORMATION: What is a Social Story™?**
>
> Social Stories™ were first developed by Carol Gray and are commonly used to support children, including those on the autistic spectrum, to understand social situations, thereby reducing their anxiety and increasing their ability to manage them. They provide information in a literal and concrete way, explaining what might happen in a particular situation and giving guidelines for behaviour.
>
> Social Stories™ should be used to focus on one behaviour at a time and should be shared with the child regularly. They can and should be adapted to the individual and their needs. It is often helpful to write them with the child.

Sharing roles and expectations in the classroom

The presence of TAs in a classroom can reduce low-level behaviour. They act as an extra pair of eyes and ears, noticing and responding to behaviours without disrupting your flow. However, doing this without exacerbating behaviour issues is not a simple matter, particularly when faced with more challenging behaviours, as so often there are issues with TA training and confidence. When TAs are insecure with the learning, they often fall back on 'policing' behaviour, as this feels like the best way to impact what is happening in the classroom.

> **Case study**
>
> Annie was working with Leo, a new TA. He was beginning to find his feet in the classroom and establish good relationships with some of his key children. When Leo had joined the school,

> he had freely admitted that he lacked confidence with maths and was not sure how he could support children with it. He had been reassured and Annie had spent extra time with him, explaining exactly what she wanted him to do in maths. Leo had seemed happy with this.
>
> However, Annie quickly noticed that her maths lessons were becoming very stressful for both her and the children, as Leo was constantly reprimanding his key children for fidgeting, fiddling and chatting, even when they weren't.
>
> Annie spoke to Leo about this. He admitted that his nervousness and desire to be supportive in these lessons might be leading him to be 'a bit tougher' than usual. It was agreed that for the time being he would not directly intervene with behaviour unless Annie asked him to do so.

Being a role model

TAs have an important role in modelling class expectations and learning. By making what they are doing explicit, your TA can make many of the implicit conventions and expectations of classroom life clearer and easier for children to follow and understand, reducing their anxiety. This can include things like:

- not talking when the teacher is talking
- joining in with talk-partner pairs to support turn-taking and helping children to stay focused
- showing a good attitude to learning – being keen and interested
- showing that it is OK and safe to make mistakes.

Setting the ground rules

Setting the ground rules is no easy matter.

- You and your TA need to work within the school's behaviour policy. This is a statutory document that ensures safety and consistency across the school, but TAs' role in behaviour management is rarely explicitly included or spelled out. This often leads to uncertainty, particularly around reward and sanction systems.

- Your school's culture will also include basic, and often unspoken, expectations, for example about how children sit, attempt activities and contribute to lessons. We tend to assume that these are obvious, but a quick tour of any school will reveal that there is a variation in implementation, even within the same year group, and rightly a clear divergence in practice in many areas – for example between Key Stage 1 and 2. This can be particularly difficult for TAs who work in multiple classes.

- Many classes establish class agreements, class contracts or charters at the beginning of the school year, often using the Rights Respecting (UNICEF) or restorative approaches. These should be revisited regularly and involve all the adults in the room, not just the children and teacher.

All these elements contribute to the 'rules' and structures you and your TA work within. These are further complicated by the need to agree how support for behaviour works within your classroom and then your respective roles and responsibilities within the system. For instance, there may be certain rewards and particular sanctions that you may not want your TA to enforce, for example asking children to move places or sending for the headteacher. If this is so, it is better to agree this before the situation arises and consider how it will be managed if you are not in the room.

> **Case study**
>
> Louis became very frustrated with Judi, his TA, as she was constantly moving children she felt were disrupting his teaching. The reality was that he found the children being moved far more disruptive than anything they had been doing. Louis knew that Judi was trying to help and did not want to tackle her on the issue directly as he knew that she would be upset.
>
> After seeking advice from the deputy head, Louis had a meeting with Judi to go through the class rules and set up a 'Classroom Contract' (see Chapter 9 for more), setting out what was expected of each of them at each stage of the lesson to ensure that the children were supported consistently.

Balancing consistency and flexibility

Schools' complex systems of rewards and sanctions, with the addition of class systems and personalised systems to support those with SEMH needs, creates a fertile ground for confusion and misunderstanding. As teachers, we implicitly understand that successful behaviour management is based in consistency imbued with flexibility. While we aspire to consistency, we understand that rigidity means that we squander time enforcing conformity and are forced to disregard the needs of many children with special needs, rather than being able to focus on supporting learning. Worst of all, we can end up penalising children for things that are part of their special needs, for example telling off children with ADHD for fidgeting, those with poor core strength for not sitting up straight or those with Tourette's for shouting out.

You and your TA need to have a shared understanding of the different systems and be clear how they apply to both the whole class and individuals, as well as the appropriate 'reasonable adjustments' for children with SEND and others, so that rewards and sanctions are applied equitably.

If this isn't working…	…try this
Arlo had ADHD and fidgeted constantly. Florence, the class TA, was constantly telling him to sit still and listen. She was particularly irritated by the fact he seemed to know the answers to his teachers' questions, despite never appearing to listen.	After a discussion with the teacher and the SENCo about ADHD, Florence began to develop a greater understanding of why Arlo fidgeted so much and that rather than inhibiting his learning, the fidgeting was in fact supporting it. Florence then researched different fiddle objects for Arlo, including kick bands to go on his chair. As she became more relaxed about his fidgeting, Arlo became less anxious, and although he continued to fiddle and doodle, it became less intrusive and disruptive.

Supporting those with SEND

Individual reward systems

Some children struggle to access a whole-school or even class reward system. They need smaller and more personalised reward systems working towards incentives that work for them, e.g. computer time, time with a particular trusted adult, drawing, reading or kicking a ball. These systems often involve children collecting visual or other tokens so that their progress is clear; something like the following example works well.

(Child's name)'s Rewards				
is working for (enter the reward)				
Reward				

For these systems to work, they depend on clear agreement between you and your TA about how and when rewards are given, possibly including recognition that there may be times when rewards are given more freely, e.g. if you feel that the child needs a break.

Identifying feelings

A key role for your TA in supporting behaviour for children with social communication difficulties and/or SEMH needs is to enable them to be able to identify and communicate about their emotions. There are many different approaches to this, such as Zones of Regulation (Kuypers, 2011). Most are based on scaling tools, which work to support children to identify their levels of anxiety and what they feel like physically as their emotions change.

	How I feel	What may help me calm
5		
4		
3		
2		
1		

Some children find it easier to use visual scales to help them identify the size of a problem that is worrying them, using animals (ant to elephant) or fruit and vegetables (pea to pumpkin) or something of particular interest to them.

Supporting with behaviour

Whatever the scale, this gives the child and adult working with them shared language to discuss the size and nature of the issue. For any of these tools to work, children need to be able to engage with an adult they trust to listen to them.

Proactive plans

Fundamental for these kinds of strategies to work is for staff to have a shared approach and consistent response to children's behaviour. One of the ways to develop this is through a proactive behaviour plan that considers how a child looks and behaves when they are calm and as their anxieties increase, and what works and does not work to help reduce their anxieties. Here's an example:

Level of anxiety	Appearance and Behaviour	Responses and actions
Calm	What they look like and how they behave?	What works to keep them like this? What leads them to escalate?
Increased anxiety	What they look like and how they behave?	What works to de-escalate the child? What leads them to escalate?
High level of anxiety	What they look like and how they behave?	What works to de-escalate the child? What leads them to escalate?
Critical incident with aggression or violence	What they look like and how they behave?	What works to de-escalate the child? What leads them to escalate?

Case study

Ismail struggled with behaviour in class. He had experienced significant domestic abuse as a toddler and showed high anxiety and attachment issues. He struggled with change and following instructions, particularly if he feared that he would not get everything right.

Despite all the work that had been done to support Ismail, Andi, one of the TAs, continued to see Ismail as 'a naughty boy' and responded to his signs of increased anxiety, such as moving around the room, scribbling and tearing up bits of paper, by telling him off. This increased his anxiety and meant that things quickly escalated into a full meltdown.

After a discussion with the headteacher and SENCo, it was agreed that all the staff who worked in the year group were invited to a meeting (for which they were paid) after school. At this meeting, they discussed Ismail. The staff shared their knowledge of Ismail to create a proactive behaviour plan, identifying what he looked like and how he acted as his levels of anxiety increased so that they could intervene and help him to calm and thus work to prevent him becoming distressed and aggressive.

Over the next few weeks, Andi became more tolerant of Ismail's behaviour and intervened less aggressively. The staff used the behaviour plan and followed the planned strategies. They were able to suggest other things that did and did not work to help Ismail calm.

These kinds of plans only need to be used for the children with a higher level of behavioural difficulties and need to be reviewed regularly to be effective.

> **Safeguarding notes:**
>
> - Keeping Children Safe in Education (DfE, 2022b) reminds us of the additional safeguarding vulnerabilities of SEND children, and that you should not assume that behaviour, mood and injuries relate to the child's condition without further exploration, as they may be indicators of possible abuse.
> - We are teachers, not mental health professionals. Neither we nor our TAs should make a medical diagnosis. We do not have qualifications to do so.
> - If you have any safeguarding concerns about a child or their behaviour, you should discuss it with your DSL.
> - You need to ensure that your TA is aware of all this.

Record keeping

Keeping records of behaviour can be a pain and time-consuming. However, it is important so that we know what we are dealing with and can identify any patterns and triggers.

> **Case study**
>
> Malachi struggled with behaviour and had frequent meltdowns where he threw objects, screamed and left the classroom. It took what felt like hours of his teacher's time

> to calm him and get him back into the classroom. When the teacher, TA and SENCo looked at the pattern of when Malachi particularly struggled with his behaviour, there was a clear pattern related to the times when he saw his mum. He lived with his grandma. While there was little that the school could do about this, it gave them information that could be used to support Malachi. This included an extra check-in with the pastoral support team on the days before he saw his mum.

Understanding the frequency and any pattern in a child's behaviour and anxieties related to specific times of the day, days of the week, people, settings or activities enables you and your TA to work together to respond to the child more effectively.

The most commonly used behaviour records are based on ABC charts, recording:

- the **A**ntecedents of the behaviour
- the **B**ehaviour
- its **C**onsequences.

There are many forms of these, for example:

Working Effectively With Your Teaching Assistant

Name						Stage on SEND register			
Date	Time	Setting	Severity (1–3)	Trigger (A)	Behaviour (B)	Others involved	Further notes (Y/N)	Actions taken (C)	Parents informed

While this kind of record is very useful, it is difficult to keep consistently. When there are many small incidents, it can be easier to use a simple blank weekly or daily timetable to record incidents. The key element is to provide a record so we are able to identify patterns and improve our support for children.

Supporting behaviour outside of the classroom

Interventions to support SEMH, pastoral and emotional needs

The majority of our TAs are responsible for supporting behaviour issues within the classroom. There are a number of specialist interventions in many schools, such as ELSA (emotional literacy support assistants), THRIVE, nurture groups and various counselling approaches, aimed at children with SEMH needs. These should involve staff with specialist training and/or experience working one-to-one or with small groups, sometimes in collaboration with outside agencies. These are both beyond the remit of most class-based TAs and this book.

However, if you have a child in your class attending one of these interventions, supporting them to attend and engage with it is a key part of your and your TA's role. Even though the lack of a clear academic focus can mean that these interventions feel disconnected from the child's classroom learning, you should try to gain an understanding of the intervention and its aims. There may be a limit to what can be shared with you to protect the child's confidentiality, particularly if outside agencies are involved.

Still, your response as children leave for and return from these sessions is key. It can be very frustrating when you are in the middle of explaining something and a child is taken out for an intervention, but it is vital that you (and any other adult in the room) suppress any irritation and are supportive about the child's departure and welcome them back.

If this isn't working…	…try this
Aadi had a history of child abuse and attended a weekly session with Ruth, the ELSA. Every time Ruth appeared in the room, Aadi would leap up and rush over to hug her and ask if it was his session time. If it wasn't, it would take Aadi sometime to resettle. Although he knew other children had sessions with Ruth, he still was upset when she took anyone else out. When it was Aadi's turn to go out with Ruth, you could guarantee that Eda, the class TA, would raise her eyebrows and make some kind of snide remark to the effect of being saved all the drama. After a few weeks of this, Aadi would just cry when Ruth came into the room and didn't want to go to his session.	It was clear that Aadi's relationship with Ruth and the work she did with him were important but the current situation was not working. Ruth and the SENCo wrote a Social Story™ to explain to Aadi that Ruth would take him for a session once a week on a Tuesday and that she also worked with other children. He was given a calendar with the day and time for his session marked on it. First Ruth shared the story with Aadi. Then Eda was asked to share the story with him each morning. This helped both Aadi and Eda understand the sessions. Ruth and the class teacher also talked to Eda about what an ELSA did, the importance of the sessions and the impact of her remarks on Aadi. Eda began to understand the impact of her remarks and body language.

TAs on the playground

Many TAs cover playground and dinner duties and have a central role in supporting and managing behaviour outside the classroom. Children demonstrate behaviours and share information at these times that they would not or could not share in the classroom. This means TAs have a key role helping you understand triggers for children's behaviours, anxieties and social interactions, which often spill from outside into the classroom.

Rightly, the majority of TA support is focused on learning time, but for many children the structure and predictability of the classroom is easier to manage than the unstructured times on the playground, in the dining hall or in school corridors, with their varied and unpredictable social interactions, movement and noise. This can be so overwhelming and anxiety-inducing, or so exciting, that some children struggle to return calmly to the classroom. Sometimes, if we can provide more support during unstructured times, children are able to arrive in lessons calmer and more able to self-regulate and access their learning independently.

This may need a change in TA deployment, so that TAs are on the playground more or they change what they do during breaks. TAs could support those who struggle with behaviour at lunches and breaktimes by:

- Setting up a quiet space on the playground with books, LEGO®, colouring, etc., for those who want space away from the bustle of the main playground.
- Providing lunchtime clubs, both 'invitation' clubs (for those who are identified as benefiting from a quiet space or structured activities) and 'open' clubs (for those who self-identify as needing this).
- Offering structured roles at breaks, including 'jobs' in the dining hall, litter patrols and gardening, for some or all of a break. Many children find that having a role gives them structure and focus for their social interactions.

- Staggered transitions, so that certain children go into class first so they can calm and settle for the afternoon without others. This may involve a 'job', e.g. getting the register, doing a calming activity or having time with you or your TA to do an emotional check-in or go through their visual timetable for the afternoon.

Case study

Vicki had a variety of medical problems that impacted her balance and meant that she became tired very quickly. Though she loved playing with her friends, she could not manage a whole lunchtime of physical play. Liv, her class TA, set up a quiet area on a bench overlooking the playground with small world play figures, books and puzzles. Vicki was able to spend some of lunchtime there with her friends. However, some of Vicki's friends struggled to stay with her as they wanted to go and play more boisterous games. This was causing tension.

At the same time, Jono, a boy in another class, was struggling with his behaviour. He quickly became overwhelmed by physical play, particularly football, often leading to aggressive behaviour. His class teacher was talking in the staffroom about her despair at finding an effective way to support him at playtimes.

Liv then suggested that he could help 'look after' Vicki and be responsible for the selection and setting up of the quiet area activities. Liv explained this role to Jono and he took to it with enthusiasm. He inducted Vicki into the world of knights and castles (one of his fascinations), which she in turn grew to love. Meanwhile Jono became calmer and more able to access the afternoon's learning.

It is important that these kinds of provisions are used to support children and not segregate them from their peers, inhibit their social interactions or be seen as a punishment. At the same time, supporting behaviour beyond the classroom can feed directly into children being more able to manage and self-regulate in the classroom.

Moving from 'won't' to 'can't'

Ultimately, the thing that makes the biggest difference to behaviour in the classroom, while being the hardest thing to manage, is changing our and our TAs' language. We need to move our discourse on from saying that children won't do something to considering that, for the vast majority of children, what we mean is that they can't. It is very hard when we are faced with a child exhibiting challenging behaviours to reframe their behaviour as anxious and/or distressed rather than aggressive and defiant. But we need to work towards reframing our language to ensure that it is supportive and that our positive interactions with children outweigh the negative ones.

Conclusion

Key to effective support for children's behaviour is to see their behaviour as communication and to respond with consistent and positive language and actions. By providing children with the security that comes from consistency imbued with flexibility, we can respond to their individual needs. To do this we need to prioritise children's wellbeing and learning over specific rules and be flexible to make reasonable adjustments to support them. For this to be effective, teachers and TAs need a shared language and understanding about behaviours and the strategies to best support them. Fundamental to making behaviour management work is the teacher/TA relationship and how it feeds into your relationships with the children. Effective support for behaviour and learning for children comes from working with trusted adults who trust each other.

Key points to remember:

- Supporting behaviour and learning should be intrinsically linked. This needs to be embedded in how you work with your TA.
- Sharing understanding of and communication about behaviour expectations is key to effective behaviour management in class.
- Behaviour strategies take time to embed, so don't expect overnight change.
- You need to look after yourself and the adults who work with you, so you can all manage behaviour effectively.

Things to discuss with senior leaders

- Is there a need and scope for support during unstructured times for some children with SEND, so that they are more able to transition back into the classroom calmly?
- What flexibility is there within the school behaviour policy to support the needs of individual pupils?

Things to think about

- How do you share your language about behaviour with your TA, so that you can mirror each other in your approach and ensure that children are receiving consistent messages?
- When children need support, such as calming activities to regulate their emotions, is this used to support them to access learning or as an alternative to learning?
- It is not always easy to challenge and discuss with your TA where there are discrepancies in your approach or language about behaviour, so how will you do this – ideally before things become an issue?

Things that work really well

- Take time to look at your school behaviour policy with your TA and check that you have a shared understanding of it and what it looks like in your classroom.
- Set a regular slot to review your behaviour records with your TA, so that you work together to identify patterns in children's behaviour; they may spot things that you do not.
- Take time for other staff and parents to share with you what strategies they find work with particular children. A simple change of wording can make a huge difference.
- Use the pupil profile from Chapter 2 to think about children's strengths and motivators, so that you can use these to support their learning and build a positive relationship with them.
- Remember that children's behaviour is not personal. All teachers have times when they find behaviour difficult. Working with others can make it easier to manage.

9 Pulling it all together by placing communication at the heart of all we do

'Working with a TA is like learning to dance. You have to learn to complement each other; sometimes it's a polished American smooth and sometimes a freestyle! It's a partnership with common goals; if that's not in place, it becomes hard work and painful for both parties and involves standing on toes!'

Teacher

This entire book could be summarised as simply 'talk and communicate'. In this final chapter, we are going to consider some key ways of supporting and structuring talk with your TA so that it is really effective and works to promote and support children's learning.

Taking on the leadership role in the classroom

Your relationship with your TA is often your first school leadership role. We are told repeatedly that teachers should retain autonomy in their classroom. The role of the TA should be to supplement, not replace the teacher. This means that you are the leader within your classroom. You are where the buck stops. Your role will include planning for learning and setting the expectations in the classroom. This needs to be shared with and include your TA so that you can work together to support the best interests of the children in your care. This can be particularly difficult for an ECT as you are still trying to develop your own professional skills and confidence, and even more so if your TA has more experience in school than you.

As in any close relationship, there are likely to be moments of tension and difficulty. Occasionally, teachers and TAs can feel that they are becoming engaged in a battle for ownership of the classroom and how things should be done. They can get to a point where one or both feel that they are constantly walking on eggshells. This is not good for anyone, including the children. If you find yourself in this situation, it is essential that you seek help from senior staff. This is not an admission of failure or that you are not managing the class successfully, but a recognition of a reality that makes teaching even more difficult.

Many schools use restorative approaches to help manage conflicts between children. The six key questions can also be supportive when responding to conflicts between adults, including you and your TA:

- What happened?
- What were you thinking?
- How did this make people feel?
- Who else has been affected?
- What should we do to put things right?
- How can we do things differently in the future?

To use these effectively often takes the mediation of a third person, either a senior leader or a trusted colleague, particularly as difficulties in teacher/TA relationships are rarely based on a single incident, but are situations that build up over time.

Classroom Contracts

Understanding the role of the different people working in the classroom is key to ensuring the consistency that children need to feel safe, which in turn will support their learning and behaviour.

This can be supported by developing a 'Classroom Contract', setting out the responsibilities of each member of the staff team in the classroom. While these may include certain common elements across a school, to be effective and useful they will be very different in Year R to Year 6. They may need to vary even across a year group. Classroom Contracts ideally need:

- To be set up as part of the common practice to support effective working at the beginning of the year, not as a response to alleviate difficulties if they arise.
- To be produced as a piece of collaborative work where all involved contribute, not regulated solely by you or your line manager. They are a way of clarifying both your and your TA's roles and the expectations around them.
- To provide a formal opportunity for all staff to ask questions, make comments and suggestions.
- To be personal to reflect the strengths of the adults and the needs of the children in your class, as well as the school policies.
- To be working documents that can be adjusted as the needs and circumstances develop, including any changes of staff and as the children mature and change during the year.
- To act as prompts for your and your TA's roles at each stage of the lesson, as well as what happens before the lesson (looking at planning) and after the lesson (feedback). You can use the five stages of the lesson discussed in Chapter 5 to support this.
- To support the focus on your TA's role in supporting learning, rather than acting as your administrative assistant.

The level of detail needed in your Classroom Contract will depend on the relationships in the classroom. If you and your TA have been working happily together for a number of years, you may need less detail than when you or your TA are new to the role. It is important to balance providing enough information to support clarity and consistency without making the Classroom Contract too long and unwieldy. Often the discussion is more important than what is recorded.

An example of a Classroom Contract could be:

Points of the lesson: Expectations, roles and responsibilities	Role of the teacher: Name	Role of the TA: Name
Before the lesson: • Any preparation needed • Sharing of planning		
Coming into the classroom and getting ready to learn: • Supporting transitions		
Giving instructions and whole-class inputs: • Active support for learning • Personalising instructions • Use of visuals		
When children are working on their own: • Prompts for learning • Who works with whom and how this is shared		
When children are working in groups: • In the classroom • Outside the classroom		

Points of the lesson: Expectations, roles and responsibilities	Role of the teacher: Name	Role of the TA: Name
At the end of the lesson: • Supporting transitions • Involvement in assessment and marking • Tidying up		
After the lesson: • Feedback		

Things to consider include:

- When and how to share planning and feedback.
- The balance of roles with the children and admin jobs, e.g. who changes reading books or marks spelling tests and when.
- Are things different at the beginning and end of the day and on different days, particularly when you have PPA?
- Any support for physical and medical needs and how these will be met.
- If there is more than one TA or teacher (due to job shares), the Classroom Contract will need to reflect and include this.
- The role of IT in the classroom, who has responsibility for this and how it is managed.
- Use of resources and particular strategies, including those used as part of behaviour management. Think about any rewards and sanction policies, including who can and can't give them, and the recording of behaviour incidents.
- The TA's role in marking – whether and how they should write in children's books.

- The hours that your TA works. They will be fewer than yours. Most TAs' contracts are term-time only and often only for school hours. They should, therefore, carry less responsibility.
- Any roles that your TA may carry out outside the classroom, e.g. playground duties, first aid, etc., and how these impact on their time in the classroom.
- If staff change, it is not always possible or appropriate just to slot a new member of staff into a role when someone leaves. The new person will have different skills, experiences and personality.

A Classroom Contract should cover class routines and set clear expectations, but it will not cover the unexpected and much of primary school life is responding to the unexpected. Within your Classroom Contract you need to retain the flexibility to respond to individual needs and situations. Equally, it cannot and should not be set in stone. You will not be able to include everything and it will need to be reviewed regularly.

If you are looking for ideas of how to work with your TA beyond this book, talk to others about what their TAs do and how they work together. Twitter and other social media provide a great source of information from people working in other schools (though don't always trust what people say on there!).

At its best, a Classroom Contract acts as a working document to support and structure discussions between you and your TA about what happens in your classroom and how you can best work as a team to support children and their learning.

Ensuring your TA has the resources they need

Related to the idea of both leadership in your classroom and a Classroom Contract is ensuring that your TA has the resources that they need to do their job effectively. These might include:

- basic stationery
- a diary or planner
- visual behaviour prompts
- cubes, number lines and other concrete resources for maths
- fiddle objects
- sticky notes
- individual whiteboards and pens
- task management boards
- a dictionary and/or thesaurus.

These will depend on the age of the children and the TA's role.

Making appraisal count

As there is no clear career structure for TAs, there is no requirement for them to have regular appraisal or line management. While many of us dread appraisal meetings and resent the paperwork involved, they are an overt recognition of the importance of our role. Appraisal is a chance to make expectations explicit and recognise and share successes, as well as an opportunity to hold staff to account. Without appraisal, TAs miss out on formal opportunities for this, particularly the recognition and celebration of their impact.

Clearly, it is important that you follow and are involved in your school's approach to TA appraisal and line management. This may mean that you are asked to do the following:

- Complete paperwork and lead the appraisal process for your TA, holding meetings with them to review their work, with or without support from someone more senior.
- Contribute, either via paperwork or more directly, to an appraisal for your TA that is led and run by someone else (e.g. the SENCo, deputy head or head of year).

- Comment on how you and your TA work together as part of your own appraisal or ECT assessments.
- Comment informally about how you work together as part of the decision-making for the next year's staff deployment.

In a few schools, there is no process of TA appraisal, however informal, or at least none that is shared with and involves them.

Whatever appraisal looks like in your school, you need to take the time at least once a term to support your TA to evaluate, and hopefully celebrate, the impact of their work, whether formally or informally. Many teachers tie these conversations in with the timetable for their own appraisal as the two conversations can helpfully feed into each other.

If you are not given a format for TA appraisal by your school, it can be helpful to consider three areas for discussion and targets:

- a focus from the school development plan, e.g. the use of effective questioning
- looking at data for a group of children your TA works with (sometimes a whole class, but more often an intervention group); this could reflect any data targets on your own appraisal, so that you are explicitly working together to achieve it
- a personal target based on an area of practice your TA wants to develop.

Whether it is an informal conversation about how things are going or a formal appraisal meeting, using the WWW (What is Working Well) and EBI (Even Better If) format for each area may help you consider successes and identify next steps, while maintaining a focus on the positive.

WWW (What is Working Well)	EBI (Even Better If)
• Mention specific things, ideally related to data or evidence in some form. Think about children's learning, SEND and EHCP targets that TAs have supported children to achieve. What are children able to do now that they were not able to do at the beginning of the appraisal period, and how did your TA contribute to that change and progress? • Remember to celebrate small and daily progress, e.g. is a child coming into school more happily, contributing to lessons more or now able to change for PE independently? Too often these things happen gradually and we forget to note them but, in many ways, they are the real markers of the impact of our TAs on children and their learning.	• Clear and specific next steps, things to change and improve. • These should be agreed between you and your TA, not something you impose on them.

Whatever the format, your comments should:

- Relate to any targets that were set at the beginning of the period.
- Be positive where possible. This is relatively easy when considering WWW, but with EBI you need to make sure that you start with a positive and develop not only what your TA but what you as a team can do to make things even better.

- Both use and review your Classroom Contract as part of the process.
- Set new targets that are SMART (Specific, Measurable, Achievable, Realistic and Timely). This means that they are relevant to their role, doable and you can measure when they have been achieved. They may relate to the targets you are set as part of your own appraisal.

The appraisal process should be part of a two-way opportunity for feedback, so that your TA is able to share their thoughts and ideas as well as being told what has happened or should happen in the classroom from your or someone else's perspective. The more you can involve them in the process, the more likely they are to be willing and able to engage in it. If they have a different perception of what is happening in the classroom, this is worth exploring.

If you can, it is worth preparing for appraisal meetings, going through and familiarising yourself with the paperwork and thinking about what you are going to say before the meeting. If you are concerned about conducting an appraisal meeting or leading the appraisal process, you should ask a senior leader for help. It can be very difficult, particularly if not all the messages you are giving are positive. You should not be left to handle difficult conversations without support.

Some further thoughts about TA appraisal

- TAs should not be held to account for things beyond their control or remit, including the impact of interventions they were not able to run or that children did not attend.
- Ensure that you identify both positives and negatives and that there is a clear link to children's learning supported by measurable data, such as whole-class data, intervention group evaluations and reviews of SEND support plans and annual reviews.
- The appraisal system should enable us to make training for TAs more focused and be linked to their needs and role in school.

By involving your TA, including in appraisal, you remind them that they are valued and you recognise their contributions to the children's learning and wellbeing, as well as holding them to account when needed.

Supporting training for your TA

Linked to appraisal should be access to training. This remains a difficult area for many TAs. Few schools are able to budget for TAs to attend training, INSET or staff meetings. This means your TA is often dependent on you for their training. A key part of this is your daily communications and sharing of what and how you are going to teach.

Providing training for your TA should not be an additional expectation. However, if you are going to use strategies and approaches that you have learned about as part of your own training or courses to change the way you teach, it is essential to share what you have learned with your TA, so you can both implement it successfully. Often, we return from training full of enthusiasm, but we need to stop and ensure that everyone working in our classrooms understands and is on board if we are going to make effective change. It can be very easy to assume that your TA knows what you know, but they don't always.

Ensuring that TAs receive training and are party to professional discussions is key to making them feel valued and involved. At times, you may need to be your TA's advocate with senior leaders, identifying and requesting training for them so that they are able to do their job effectively. Senior leaders are not always aware of the strengths and areas of development for TAs, as they don't work directly with them. When offering TAs training, we need to be aware of the hours they work. Many are happy to be involved in this through goodwill, but this should not be an expectation.

In an ideal world, you and your TA would be able to access training together so that you could work collaboratively to implement it.

When this is not possible, you both need to try to share your learning so that you can use it to support the children and each other.

If you want your TA to develop their practice, they will need support and training (either formally or informally). Just hoping they will pick up what you are doing and change their practice rarely works!

Conclusion

As the teacher, you are responsible for your class and their learning. You are the leader in your classroom. Your TA's role is to promote inclusion. We need to be careful that this does not become exclusion as a child becomes separated from their peers or you, their teacher. This means that the TA's primary role should be in the classroom working with a range of children, so that you also work with all the children in your class.

To support this, you and your TA need to be clear about your roles and how you work best together as a team. As we have seen, this often needs the roles in the classroom to be discussed, explained and formalised. A Classroom Contract can be a useful vehicle to do this. It allows us to stop, think about and discuss what we are doing in our classroom. The process of reflection and review improves our practice. This can be further supported by structured appraisal for your TA and focused training for you both.

Ten key take aways from this book

We started this book talking about 'sharing the cape' and the ten challenges to effective TA/teacher relationships. As we finish, we aim to work to enable all the adults in our classrooms to feel that they have an integral role in working to promote the learning of the whole class, not just supporting an individual child. To achieve this, your TA needs to be involved in the planning, delivery and organisation of the learning for all the children in your class. You need to aim to work as a team – 'sharing the cape' and valuing all the staff's contributions to support and promote children's learning.

1. **The children need to be at the heart of everything that you do in your classroom**. You and your TA need to understand the boundaries of your relationship with the children and each other. These should be professional working relationships. You might be friends with your TA, but you don't have to be. Your and your TA's relationship is about **promoting and supporting children's learning**, not the reason you are there.
2. **Relationships** are vital but take time to form. Ups and downs in them are part of life. Having structures and systems to support working relationships, such as Classroom Contracts, can make things clearer and easier to manage.
3. We need to value and give time to communication with our TAs – sharing planning, feedback and information about the children – as a two-way process. **Effective communication** takes time and needs to be given priority if it is to be successful and useful.
4. Your TA should be working within the classroom and throughout the lesson to support learning. This needs to be more than repeating instructions, so to support learning effectively your TA needs **an understanding of the curriculum**. They need to be able to prompt children for independence, working to avoid them becoming prompt-dependent.
5. Your TA should supplement and not replace you. All children, including those with SEND, are entitled to quality teacher time as well as TA support. This can be supported through **a 'key person' approach**. We need to be conscious of the risk that a high level of TA support can lead to children becoming 'separated' from either their teacher and/or peers.
6. Putting in **the correct support for children's learning** is often time-consuming. However, many of the best interventions

and supports are small tweaks and adaptations to quality-first teaching throughout all five phases of the lesson.

7. We need to invest time in order to save time by **focusing on the development of children's skills**, not task completion in a single lesson.

8. **Successful support for behaviour and learning** is intrinsically interlinked. If you can get one right, it will support the other.

9. Your TA can support and **enhance your communications with parents** but should not become a replacement for you in these key communications. To support your children effectively, you need to build a triangle of trust around them that includes their parents and your TA as well as you. This needs to recognise, share and value your different perspectives.

10. Stop and **consider what has gone well**, so that you can identify positives in how you and your TA work together. It is too easy to focus on the negatives and miss the differences you make for the children in your care.

Glossary

APDR cycle	Assess, Plan, Do, Review cycle
CAMHS	Child and adolescent mental health services
DHT	Deputy head teacher
DISS	The Deployment and Impact of Support Staff study
DSL	Dedicated safeguarding lead
EAL	English as an additional language
ECT	Early career teacher
EEF	Education Endowment Foundation
EHCP	Education health and care plans
ELKAN	Specialist speech and language programmes
ELSA	Emotional literacy support assistant
EP	Educational psychologist
EYFS	Early Years Foundation Stage
HLTA	Higher level teaching assistant
HSLW	Home school link worker
IEP	Individual education plan
INSET	In-service training
ISP	Individual support plan
LSA	Learning support assistant

MITA	Maximising the Impact of Teaching Assistants: an educational project based at the Institute of Education in London, looking at the deployment and impact of TAs
Ofsted	Office for Standards in Education, Children's Services and Skills: the organisation that carries out school inspections in England
OT	Occupational therapist
PE	Physical education
PP	Pupil premium
PPA	Planning, preparation and assessment: time out of the classroom given to teachers to complete these activities following the National Agreement in 2003
SALT	Speech and language therapy/ist
SEMH	Social, emotional and mental health needs
SENCo	Special educational needs coordinator (sometimes called a SENDCo – special educational needs and Disabilities co-ordinator)
SEND	Special education needs and disabilities
SLT	Senior leadership team
SMART targets	Specific, Measurable, Achievable, Realistic and Timely
TA	Teaching assistant
THRIVE	A strategic approach to whole-school emotional health and wellbeing
WPR	Wider pedagogical role model: issues of preparedness, deployment and practice

References

ATL, DFES, GMB, NAHT, NASUWT, NEOST, PAT, SHA, TGWU, UNISON and WAG (2003), Raising standards and tackling workload: A national agreement: Time for standards. [online] Available at: https://dera.ioe.ac.uk/540/1/081210thenationalagreementen.pdf.

Carol Gray Social Stories (n.d.), Hompage. [online] Available at: https://carolgraysocialstories.com.

Carter, G. and Coleman, M. (2020), *Colourful Semantics: A resource for developing children's spoken and written language skills*. London: Routledge, Taylor & Francis Group.

Cozens, J.A. (2014), *Appreciating the contribution of teaching assistants (TAs): A study of TAs' descriptions of their support for pupils identified as having special educational needs and disabilities (SEND), using an appreciative inquiry (AI) approach*, D.Ed.Psych thesis, University of Birmingham.

Department for Education (DfE) (2011), Teachers' Standards. [online] Available at: https://assets.publishing.service.gov.uk/government/uploads/system/uploads/attachment_data/file/1040274/Teachers__Standards_Dec_2021.pdf.

Department for Education (DfE) (2015a), Special educational needs and disability code of practice: 0 to 25 years. [online] Available at: https://assets.publishing.service.gov.uk/government/uploads/system/uploads/attachment_data/file/398815/SEND_Code_of_Practice_January_2015.pdf.

Department for Education (DfE) (2015b), Statistical first release: School workforce in England: November 2014. [online] Available at: https://assets.publishing.service.gov.uk/government/uploads/system/uploads/attachment_data/file/440577/Text_SFR21-2015.pdf.

Department for Education (DfE) (2019a), Early Career Framework. [online] Available at: https://assets.publishing.service.gov.uk/government/uploads/system/uploads/attachment_data/file/978358/Early-Career_Framework_April_2021.pdf.

Department for Education (DfE) (2019b), ITT Core Content Framework. [online] Available at: https://assets.publishing.service.gov.uk/government/uploads/system/uploads/attachment_data/file/974307/ITT_core_content_framework_.pdf.

Department for Education (DfE) (2021), Statutory framework for the Early Years Foundation Stage. [online] Available at: https://assets.publishing.service.gov.uk/government/uploads/system/uploads/attachment_data/file/974907/EYFS_framework_-_March_2021.pdf.

Department for Education (DfE) (2022a), SEND review: Right support, right place, right time. [online] Available at: www.gov.uk/government/consultations/send-review-right-support-right-place-right-time.

Department for Education (DfE) (2022b), Keeping children safe in education. [online] Available at: https://assets.publishing.service.gov.uk/government/uploads/system/uploads/attachment_data/file/1101454/Keeping_children_safe_in_education_2022.pdf.

Early Years Coalition (2021), Birth to 5 matters: Non-statutory guidance for the Early Years Foundation Stage. [online] Available at: www.birthto5matters.org.uk/wp-content/uploads/2021/04/Birthto5Matters-download.pdf.

Education Act (1981), UK. [online] Available at: www.legislation.gov.uk/ukpga/1981/60/enacted.

Education Endowment Foundation (EEF) (2018), Making best use of teaching assistants. [online] Available at: https://educationendowmentfoundation.org.uk/education-evidence/guidance-reports/teaching-assistants.

Education Endowment Foundation (EEF) (2021a), Making best use of teaching assistants: A self-assessment guide. [online] Available at: https://educationendowmentfoundation.org.uk/public/files/Publications/Teaching_Assistants/TA_RAG_self-assessment.pdf.

Education Endowment Foundation (EEF) (2021b), Teaching and Learning Toolkit. Available at: https://educationendowment foundation.org.uk/education-evidence/teaching-learning-toolkit.

Education Policy Institute (2020), Understanding school revenue expenditure: Part 5: Expenditure on teaching assistants. [online] Available at: https://epi.org.uk/publications-and-research/unders

tanding-school-revenue-expenditure-part-5-expenditure-on-teaching-assistants.

Elklan (n.d.), Training to support children's language and learning. [online] Available at: www.elklan.co.uk.

Equality and Human Rights Commission (2015), Reasonable adjustments for disabled pupils: Guidance for schools in England [online] Available at: www.equalityhumanrights.com/sites/default/files/reasonable_adjustments_for_disabled_pupils_1.pdf.

Giangreco, M.F. (2021), Maslow's hammer: Teacher assistant research and inclusive practices at a crossroads. *European Journal of Special Needs Education*, 36, (2), 278–293.

Ginni, S., Pestell, G., Mason, E. and Knibbs, S. (2018), Newly qualified teachers: Annual survey 2017. [online] Available at: https://assets.publishing.service.gov.uk/government/uploads/system/uploads/attachment_data/file/738037/NQT_2017_survey.pdf.

GOV.UK (2021), School workforce in England: Reporting year 2019. [online] Available at: https://explore-education-statistics.service.gov.uk/find-statistics/school-workforce-in-england.

Kuypers, L. (2011), The Zones of Regulation: A concept to foster self-regulation and emotional control. [online] Available at: www.zonesofregulation.com/index.html.

Maximising the Impact of Teaching Assistants (MITA) (2021), Homepage. [online] Available at: https://maximisingtas.co.uk/impact.php.

Nash, M. (2014), *Teachers and teaching assistants working together: The perceptions of teaching assistants within a national framework*, D.Ed thesis, Manchester Metropolitan University.

Ofsted (2022), School inspection handbook: Section 8. [online] Available at: www.gov.uk/government/publications/section-8-school-inspection-handbook-eif/school-inspection-handbook-section-8.

Restorative Justice Council (n.d.), Restorative practice in education. [online] Available at: https://restorativejustice.org.uk/restorative-practice-education-0.

Restorative Justice 4 Schools (n.d.), Homepage. [online] Available at: www.restorativejustice4schools.co.uk/wp/?page_id=45.

Sharples, J., Webster, R. and Blatchford, P. (2018), Making best use of teaching assistants: Guidance report. Education Endowment Foundation.

[online] Available at: https://maximisingtas.co.uk/assets/content/taguidancereportmakingbestuseofteachingassisstants.pdf.

Skipp, A., Hopwood, V. and Ask Research (2019), Deployment of teaching assistants in schools: Research report. Department for Education. [online] Available at: https://assets.publishing.service.gov.uk/government/uploads/system/uploads/attachment_data/file/812507/Deployment_of_teaching_assistants_report.pdf.

Sobel, D. and Alston, S. (2021) *The Inclusive Classroom: A new approach to differentiation*. London: Bloomsbury.

The Warnock Report (1978) Special Educational Needs: Report of the Committee of Enquiry into the Education of Handicapped Children and Young People. London: HMSO. [online] Available at: www.educationengland.org.uk/documents/warnock/warnock1978.html

Thrive (n.d.), Free mental health lead training. [online] Available at: www.thriveapproach.com/freetraining?gclid=CjwKCAjwkMeUBhBuEiwA4hpqEJWGdfJ4RrBIG6-Vum7-Zc3xILY8i-d5mrHeXajA_3BDOVkKuyYECBoCYLkQAvD_BwE.

UNICEF (2016), Rights Respecting schools. [online] Available at: www.unicef.org.uk/rights-respecting-schools.

UNISON, NAHT, NET, MPTA, MITA and RTSA (2016), Professional standards for teaching assistants: Advice for headteachers, teachers, teaching assistants, governing boards and employers. [online] Available at: www.skillsforschools.org.uk/media/1078/ta-standards-final-june2016-1.pdf.

Webster, R., Bosanquet, P., Franklin, S. and Parker, M. (2021), *Maximising the Impact of Teaching Assistants: A practical guide for school leaders*. London: Routledge.

Index

ABC charts 187–189
anxieties 31, 52, 71, 116, 176, 184, 187
appraisal 13, 203–207
appreciation, of TA tasks 24–26
Assess, Plan, Do, Review cycle 60–61, 167
awesomeness book 128

behaviour management 176–177
　anxiety 176
　in classroom 172–173
　focus difficulties 175
　iceberg model 173
　impact on 171–172
　records keeping 186–188
　transitions 174
behaviour policy document 179

calm boxes 176
calm time 176
catch-up sessions 134
Classroom Contract 22–23, 180, 198–202
classroom learning
　children's independence in 93–95
　differentiation in 106
　effective questioning 100–101
　and interventions 136–137
　from mistakes 96
　scaffolding 97–98
　sensory issues in 104–105
　space sharing and positioning of TAs 98–100
　teachers' and TAs' role, difference in 91–93
　visual prompts usage 102–104
communication with TAs
　children related 154–156
　effective 31–33
　feedback sharing 164–169
　issues in 158–159
　language for 156
　learning intentions and 161
　and outcome of children 161
　planning lessons 157
　shared understanding in 156–157
　sharing planning 164
　subject knowledge issues in 162–163
　teaching slides 160
　time setting for 154
　and vocabulary 161
　see also home–school communications
conflicts management 198
costings 62
cut away concept 40–41

Department for Education (DfE) 3
Deployment and Impact of Support Staff (DISS) study 17
differentiated learning 106, 118, 135, 137
　see also classroom learning

EAL (English as an additional language) 22

early career teachers (ECTs) 31
Early Years Foundation Stage (EYFS)
    framework 23, 164
Early Years support 23–24
EBI (Even Better If) format 204–205
echo teaching 134
Education Act (1981) 5
Education Endowment Foundation
    (EEF) 17, 139
education, health and care plan
    (EHCP) 6, 45
emotional literacy support assistant
    (ELSA) 134
emotional support 128

feedback 168–169
    Assess, Plan, Do, Review
        cycle 167
    of children with SEND 168
    and Early Years Colleagues 164
    forms for 165
    level of support for 164–165
    useful and less useful 166–167
    valuable 33–34
fiddle objects 104–105, 175, 181
flip chart 115
flipping roles 40
flow chart 115
focus difficulties 175

general class TA 22
Gray, Carol 177
group interactions 124–127

helicopter approach 49–51
higher level teaching assistants
    (HLTAs) 13
home-grown interventions
    140–142
home–school communications
    books 83

face-to-face communication 72
formal communication 71–72
informal communication 72
information-sharing 80–81
key person approach 75–76
out-of-school relationships 86–88
record system for 81–83
support staffs for 73
TA involvement in 73–74, 78–80
and trust 77
verbal communications 86
written communications 83–86
see also communication with TAs;
    supporting children with SEND

iceberg model, of behaviour
    management 173
'if…then…' boards 174
Inclusive Classroom, The 109
individual classroom
    arrangements 29
individual education plans (IEPs) 62
individual support plans (ISPs) 62
instructions, delivering and
    receiving 114–117
interventions specialists 22,
    134, 189
interventions
    and classroom learning 136–137
    conditions for best 139
    evidence-based 140–142
    home-grown 140–142
    inside classroom 133, 137–138
    issues in 145
    leading 144
    outside agencies or specialists
        for 144
    outside classroom
        (outventions) 134
    over-learning 147
    pre-learning 145–147

for SEND children 135
timetabling 142–144
ITT Core Content Framework 3
IT usage 122–123

job insecurity 11–12

Keeping Children Safe in Education 186
key person approach 56–57, 75–76

liaison time of TAs, lack of 15–17
learning vocabulary, elements in 146–147
lesson, supporting
  classroom, leaving 129
  concrete resources 120
  differentiated learning 118
  emotional support 128
  entering classroom 110–111
  focussed interventions 113
  group interactions 124–127
  IT usage 122–123
  learning, finishing 128
  marking 128
  observations focus 117, 127
  oral rehearsal 116–117
  recording 121
  scribing 121–122
  self-talk 124
  short-term rewards 124
  task management board 119–120
  teacher input instructions 114–115
  visual support 114
  visual timetables 111–113
  voice-activated software 123
live marking 165
lunches and break times 191

management of TAs 2–3
  effective usage of TAs 3
  relationships building 3–4
  support provided by TAs 3
  support staff deployment 3
Maslow's hammer approach 65
Maximising the Impact of Teaching Assistants (MITA) project 11, 17, 139
meeting and greeting 110–111
mind reading 32
movement breaks 53, 93, 104, 105, 134, 176

National Agreement, The 7
National Curriculum 7
non-pedagogical tasks 7, 24
now and next cards 52, 93, 118, 174
nurture groups 134, 145, 189

observations 117, 128
observer, TAs as 127
occupational therapy 134
oops card 112–113
opportunities for proving strengths 36–38

paraprofessional responsibilities 12
PE lessons 134
personal, social, health and economic education (PSHE) 143
playgrounds 191–193
policing behaviour 177
pre-learning 134, 145–147, 175
proactive behaviour plan 184–186
progress 60–64
  documents 62–63
  evidence 61–62
pupil profile
  template 57–58

quality-first teaching 48, 134

recording learning 81–83, 121–123, 186–189
relationship with TAs
　appraisal 203–207
　Classroom Contract 22–23, 179, 198–199
　classroom resources 202–203
　conflicts management 198
　leadership in classroom 197
　trainings 207–208
　see also communication with TAs
relationships and sex education (RSE) 143
respecting knowledge 35–36
reward systems 179–182
role modelling 178

self-talk 124
SEMH (social, emotional and mental health) 8, 22, 93, 134, 142, 180, 182, 189
SEN Support level 6, 45
SENCo 6
SEND children
　and anxieties 184
　classroom support for 51
　communication language 193
　differentiated curriculum for 135
　and emotions 182
　helicopter approach 49–51
　inclusion of 18–19, 48–49
　key person approach for 56–57, 75–76
　maximising learning time 48
　one-to-one support 45
　outside classroom 189–193
　progress documents 62–63
　progress evidence 61–62
　progress identification 60–64

pupil profile template 57–58
quality-first teaching 48
reasonable adjustments for 180–181
resources for 52–53
reward systems 181–182
support interventions 5–6, 144
targets 62
team building for 54–56, 59–60, 86
triangle of trust for 69–70, 77
Velcro® approach 49–51
SEND Code of Practice 6, 45, 47, 62
SEND support contract 22–23
sensory circuits 176
short-term rewards 124
'side-lined' children, including 38–41
SMART (specific, measurable, achievable, realistic and timely) targets 206
Sobel, Daniel 109
Social Stories™ 177
sticky notes 166
swap roles 37–38

TA roles
　changes in 4–7
　establishing 29–31
　lack of clarity on 14–15
　multiple 7–9
　understanding 21–24
task management boards 52, 119–120
teacher/TA working relationship 30–31
Teachers' Standards (Standard 8) 3, 12
teaching slides 160, 175
thanking TAs 34–35
THRIVE 134, 189

timetabling 142–144
time warnings 128
training, lack of 12–15
transitions, and behaviour management 174
triangle of trust 69–70, 77

Velcro®'TA model 49–51, 54–56, 76
verbal communications 86
visual behaviours 173
visual checklist 128
visual prompts 102–104, 147, 175
visual scales 182–184
visual timetables 52, 84, 93, 111–113, 174, 192
voice-activated software 123

Warnock Report 5, 18
weekly rotation of groups 39
whiteboard 90, 103, 115, 175
whole-school deployment decisions 27–28
whole-school guidance 28–29
Wider Pedagogical Role model (WPR) 18
worked examples 52–53
written checklist 128
written communications 83–86
WWW (What is Working Well) format 204–205

Zones of Regulation 182
zoning classroom 41

Praise for *Working Effectively With Your Teaching Assistant*

'A comprehensive and accessible guide to support anyone in gaining the most from their support staff. I enjoyed the many practical strategies and case studies to support and inspire!'

Andy Taylor, Senior Lecturer at University of Worcester, @MrTs_NQTs

'Sara uses her wealth of experience to share a solution-focused approach to working with TAs. There is great insight into how to positively develop practices that support the efficacy of TAs in schools.'

Kenny Wheeler, SEND, Inclusion and Leadership Consultant, @KennyInclusion

'A must for teachers, SENCOs and TAs alike. Whilst clearly EYFS and Primary focused, it works for Secondary schools too. The advice, guidance and examples are practical, realistic and accessible.'

Dr Hélène Cohen, lecturer, SEND consultant, tutor/supervisor for NASENCO/iSENDCO Masters awards, @EdPleaseMiss

'An absolute gem! It's a book that every teacher should read if they want to get the absolute best from their TA. Full of practical strategies which can be easily implemented.'

Carmel Martin, Deputy Headteacher and SENDCo

'At last, a guide to support teachers in how to direct the adults who support in their classrooms. Thank you Sara! The thinking and research that has gone into this book is phenomenal! This research informed guide covers every operational element of classroom practice, legislation, teacher standards and everything that could possibly be conceived about the education of primary children is included.

'Whether you are a newly qualified teacher or an educator who has been teaching for many years, this book is for you. Teaching assistants are part of the educational tapestry of schools, interwoven into the daily timetable. Therefore, it is essential that teachers know best how to work with the supporting adults in their classrooms. This book provides this valuable information for senior leaders and teachers, how to deploy and work effectively with the teaching assistants within the primary classroom. Every school should purchase a copy. Every PGCE and ECT professional development course should feature Sara Alston's work.'

Aimee Durning MBE, Co-Founder of the UK TA Network Hub and Director of Inclusion and Community at the University of Cambridge Primary School

'Practical, highly relatable advice for new and experienced teachers with brilliant personal stories and case studies that really brings this book alive. The key takeaways at the end of each chapter are succinct and support teachers with knowing exactly what to do next to consolidate and improve outcomes in their class. Teachers learn to teach; nobody teaches teachers about managing TAs, this book gives a superb step-by-step guide to support best practice.'

Kiren Bennett, SLE SEND, Assistant Headteacher for Inclusion at Ulverley School, part of Robin Hood MAT

'This well-informed book is an important must-read for anyone teaching alongside an assistant. This relationship can be confusing, so this book unpicks issues through a case study approach and common sense thinking.'

Dr Sue Allingham, Consultant, Author, Trainer, @DrSue22

'Packed with tried-and-tested advice from a life of coordinating SEN, Sara's book is my new "go-to". Highly recommend.'

Ben Slater, Founder and Lead Consultant, Fiveways Devon, @DevonFiveways

About the Author

Sara Alston is passionate about achieving the best for all children and ensuring that 'the welfare of the child is paramount' remains at the heart of all that is done in schools. She promotes these beliefs through her work as a SENCo and an independent SEND and safeguarding consultant and trainer.

As a consultant, she works to support schools, including those who are 'under-SENCoed' to develop outstanding SEND practice. She conducts TA, SEND and safeguarding reviews. Sara is becoming a regular speaker at conferences and leads school INSET and training events for a range of SEND and safeguarding issues.

Sara has written a range of courses and resources for teachers and TAs for a number of organisations, including The Key, Inclusion Expert, School Bus and UK Parliament Education Service. She writes regular articles for *Teach Primary* and *Headteacher Update*, as well as blogs about SEND and safeguarding issues. With Daniel Sobel, Sara wrote *The Inclusive Classroom: A new approach to differentiation* (published January 2021), which was a finalist for ERA Education Book of the Year 2022.

She is a contributor to *Tiny Voices Talks* edited by Toria Bono and *It Takes 5 years to Become a Teacher* by Ros Wilson.

Sara is the proud mum of two adult sons and lives with a rather grumpy black and white cat.

If you want to read more by the same author…

*The Inclusive Classroom:
A new approach to differentiation*

By Daniel Sobel and Sara Alston

Effective inclusion in the classroom shouldn't be a burden; it should be the most rewarding aspect of a teacher's role.

> 'An excellent guide to changing approaches to inclusion and creating a culture where all children can flourish.'
>
> *SEN Magazine*

In this innovative guide to supporting the most vulnerable students, experts Daniel Sobel and Sara Alston help primary and secondary teachers understand the barriers to children's learning. Emphasising the importance of meeting needs rather than focusing on diagnosis, they provide proven adaptive teaching methods that maximise learning for the whole class.

Guiding teachers through all the different phases of a single lesson, from starters to plenaries, the unique format of *The Inclusive Classroom* will help bring inclusion to the forefront of any lesson plan. Each chapter contains simple, effective actions to differentiate and improve learning outcomes for students vulnerable to underachievement, including those traditionally labelled SEN, EAL, pupil premium, looked after and young carers. Also provided are back-up ideas for when things don't go to plan, real-life anecdotes from teachers, and instructions on how to rethink traditional diagnoses and instead prioritise strengths and participation needs.

Available to purchase at www.bloomsbury.com/uk/, where you can also view an extract from inside the book!